AF505466

Michael Craig-Martin Present Sense

Michael Craig-Martin

WINDSOR

**Royal
Academy
of Arts**

Present Sense

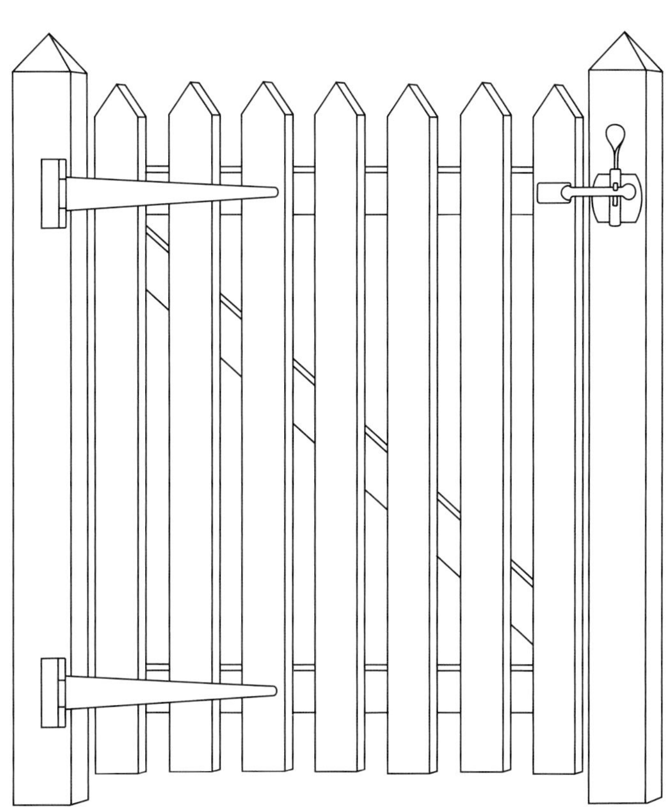

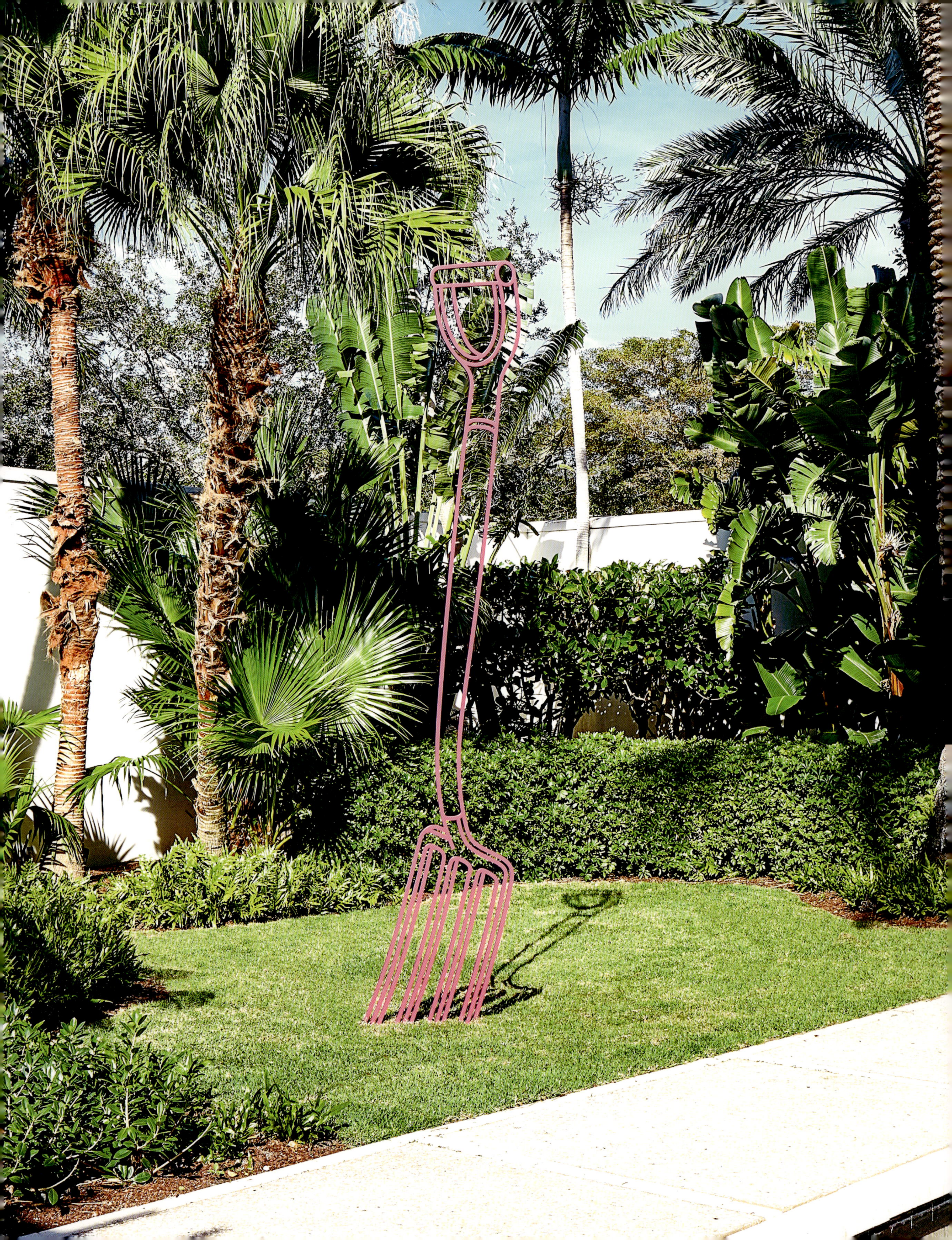

Foreword

We are delighted to welcome to The Gallery at Windsor an exhibition devoted to the recent work of internationally renowned British artist, Sir Michael Craig-Martin RA. He will exhibit paintings and editions in the gallery, simultaneously with an exhibition of his sculpture installed in the landscape at Windsor.

The exhibition *Present Sense* is the second in our three-year collaboration with the Royal Academy of Arts, and working with this major conceptual artist is an exciting continuation of the world-class programming which takes place every year at The Gallery.

It is the first time we have invited an artist to show their three-dimensional works outdoors here. When I visited Michael's studio with my husband Galen over eighteen months ago I was struck by the scale and the simplicity of his giant, colourful sculptures. I knew they would look wonderful at Windsor, and that their presence would involve our Members and guests, on a daily basis, in the cultural endeavours of The Gallery.

We extend a warm thank you to Christopher Le Brun, the President of the Royal Academy, a distinguished painter who has exhibited here at Windsor, and to Tim Marlow, the Royal Academy's Artistic Director, for their advice and guidance. Thanks also to curator Hannah Freedberg and her team at Gagosian, London, and to Alan Cristea who has collaborated with Michael on editions for many years and lends prints and a new light box to this exhibition. Thanks also to Ben Luke, the art critic and writer, for his enlightening essay.

I would like to acknowledge Jane Smalley and Laura Kelley and the dedicated and committed staff at Windsor who work tirelessly to realise these exhibitions. I would also like to thank Nicola Togneri for coordinating this series of exhibitions and the staff at the RA who are supporting us through this exciting project.

At last, my warmest thank you goes to Sir Michael, my fellow country-man and artist of such great integrity, for bringing his thought-provoking works to all of us at Windsor.

The Hon. Hilary M. Weston, CM, CVO, OOnt

Garden Fork (magenta), 2017

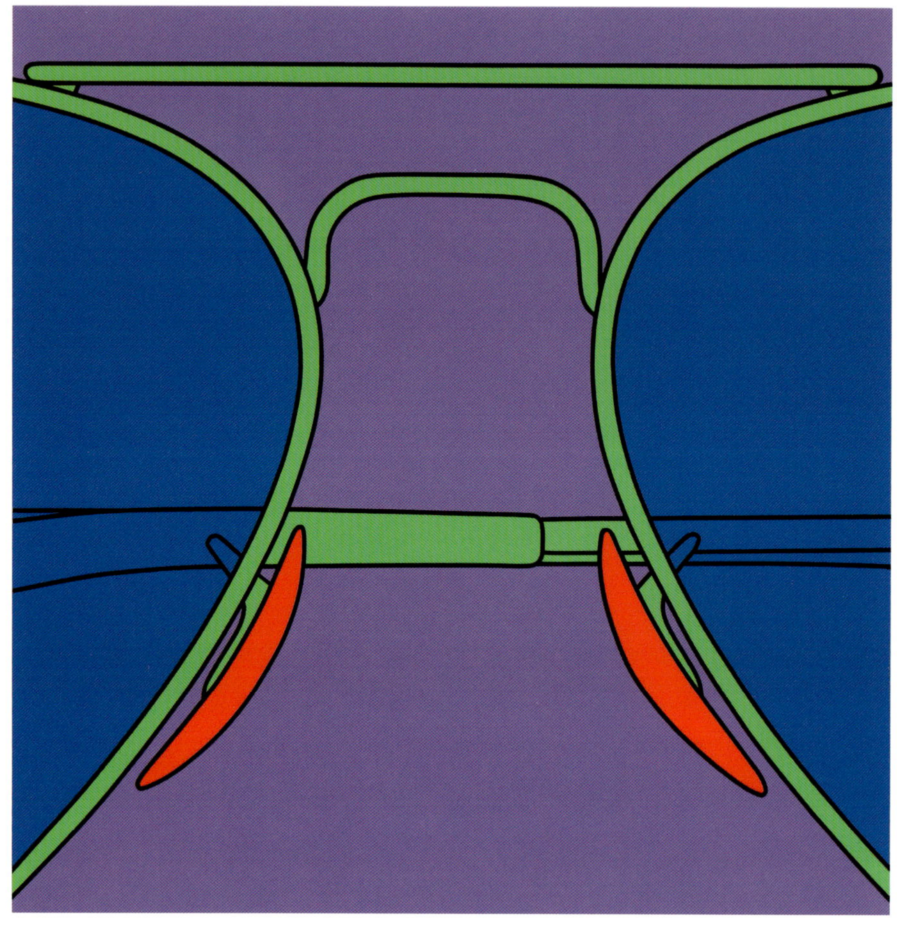

Untitled (sunglasses fragment), 2017
Acrylic on aluminium, 24 × 24 in. (60 × 60 cm)

Christopher Le Brun PRA

The Royal Academy of Arts
and The Gallery at Windsor:
A Curatorial Partnership

In collaboration with Hilary Weston, Creative Director of The Gallery at Windsor, and Tim Marlow, Artistic Director at the Royal Academy of Arts, we devised a three-year programme of exhibitions in Florida by leading Royal Academicians. The exhibitions take place from January to April, 2018 to 2020.

This is the second year of our curatorial partnership, and in addition to the exhibitions series, our internationally acclaimed Royal Academy Learning department is bringing its wealth of experience to advise on all aspects of the educational programming. The Gallery is at the heart of a warmly receptive community of international residents; it has a very active outreach programme in the locality and receives visitors from across the state of Florida and beyond.

Representatives from the Royal Academy experienced a generous welcome at the first exhibition in Florida in January 2018, and we were delighted to receive a cohort from Windsor at the 250th Royal Academy Summer Exhibition in London in June. This group also visited the London studio of the next artist to exhibit at Windsor – sworn to secrecy until the exhibition was announced – and saw paintings in progress which are now a central feature of this major presentation of his work.

Sir Michael Craig-Martin is a principal figure in international conceptual art, and a highly respected member of the British art establishment, whether as a board member and advisor, or as teacher and lecturer. During his time at Goldsmiths' College in the 1990s, he educated a generation of students who would become known as the Young British Artists, or YBAs. More recently when he was co-ordinator of the acclaimed 2015 Royal Academy Summer Exhibition, his vision and revitalisation of its presentation led to record attendance and sales, and a reappraisal of the exhibition's position as an important event in the contemporary art calendar.

With refined understatement, Craig-Martin's unmistakable drawn images seem to encapsulate a universal modern visual culture. They are visible in the recent paintings, sculptures and prints that make up this exhibition. It is rare to have the opportunity to see so many of his sculptures simultaneously, and seems an apt celebration of Windsor's thirtieth anniversary to show works in the grounds for the first time, where these monumental 'drawings' will draw visitors into the extraordinary landscape.

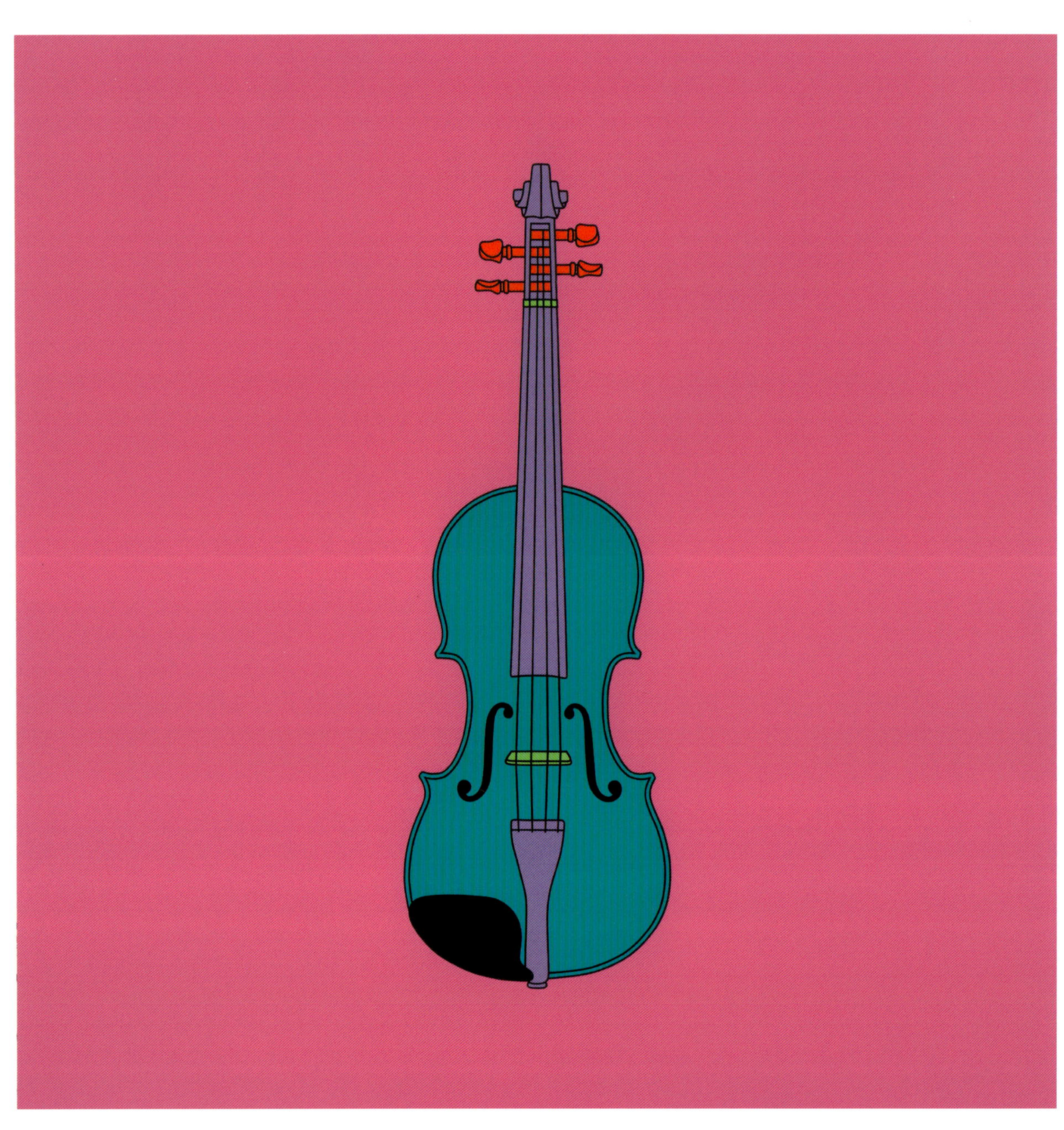

Untitled (violin), 2013
Acrylic on aluminium, 78¾ × 78¾ in. (200 × 200 cm)

Michael Craig-Martin in Conversation with Tim Marlow

Tim Marlow: Michael, I know you have shown extensively across the globe, and I presumed you had shown a lot in America, but it turns out you haven't. So how do you feel about showing at Windsor in Florida?

Michael Craig-Martin: I am very excited by the prospect as it presents an opportunity to bring sculpture, painting and printmaking together for the first time. I have been able to choose the placement of each sculpture in the grounds, which are grand and varied: you'll see one and then walk a while and come across another.

Do sculpture, painting and printmaking lead to fundamentally different approaches, or are you exploring the same territory through different media?

Over the years I've found that what started as a way of drawing has become a language. What is interesting is to try to explore ways of using that language to address different things. What I deal with in the paintings is different to what I deal with in the sculpture; what I address in prints is different to what I do in the paintings. They're all part of the same dialogue but they each allow a different focus or emphasis.

So it's the language of images but in different media.

Yes, the images are the same in the prints as the sculptures or paintings. But the thing about having my own visual language is that the meaning can change: the same image can be used to mean something different by changing the context in which it is used.

Some people talk about the banality of everyday images, but when I hear you talk about your work you make interesting historical parallels. You're not necessarily saying that a pair of sunglasses is as culturally resonant as a fragment of a classical temple dug up in Rome, but you talk about an equivalence between objects from the past and objects from the present.

I've always drawn everything exactly the same way, in order to remove the classifications or hierarchies. A violin is understandably seen as a valuable and exquisite object, while the paper cup your coffee comes in or a coat hanger that comes with clothes from the dry cleaners has no value at all. Some things are seen as precious, but in my language they all have the same value. I'm trying to eliminate the normal distinctions, so you look at one thing in the same way as you look at another thing, and give equal weight, equal importance.

There is also the idea about what we value culturally that is evident in the objects you select – what remains as the trace of a particular culture and what disappears. Are you systematic in the way you select things or is this something that just happens over time? After ten years the cassette, as you depicted it, becomes redundant.

It never occurred to me in the beginning, when my idea of ordinary objects was a table, chair, book, shoe, hammer, screwdriver. When I started making these drawings, I thought there were going to be tens of thousands of things to draw; I was shocked to discover that it's much more limited because so many things are variations. I like drawing chairs, there must be half a million kinds and yet each one is identifiable as a 'chair'. You look at any one of them and say 'chair' – not 'a kind of chair'. The objectness of the object stays constant while the things that surround it are so variable. I go for things that are iconic, that sum something up. There are telephones that look like cats but I don't draw them.

Famously, you put a glass of water on a shelf and titled it *An Oak Tree* [1973]. There's a gap between the labels that we give objects and the things themselves. Through consensus we acknowledge that what we call a chair has four legs, therefore why not call a glass of water an oak tree?

My curiosity about the relationship between an object and an image of the object is that the image of the object does not physically look like the object from which it was taken. A picture of a chair doesn't look anything like a chair, it isn't made out of the same stuff, it's flat, it's only a couple of lines, maybe a bit of colour. And yet this miracle happens – we experience the presence of an object that is absent. In other words, a drawing of a chair is not a chair; I see this in a general sense as equivalent to the relationship I indicated between the glass of water and an oak tree.

So we talk about the language of things, and you might say the language of things and the language of images are opposite sides of the same coin.

Yes, one of the things I realised is that in the history of art, right from the cave paintings, people have made images of things because images allow you to have the object but to have a degree of flexibility that the object itself will not allow. You can make an image of an object gigantic or tiny in relation to the real thing; you can make it blue or green; you could make it do things; you can put it into context. An image has an expressive range.

The objects depicted in your paintings and prints and sculptures, are they generic, are they specific, are they from your imagination?

I never draw anything that isn't from a specific single object. If I'm using a photograph, I use one photograph. I'm not seeking to draw a generalisation, except that the example of it could ultimately be seen as representing the general field of that object. My images exist somewhere between the particular and the general, an area in between.

That is a beautiful description in a different way, I think, of your sculptures, which are both not objects but objects; they're not the object depicted, they are sculptural objects and they are images. They evaporate from one perspective, hovering between being solid and transparent, between line and form. As you walk around them, they become a single line.
Yes, and the image completely disappears. They have turned out to be a wonderful expression of language ambiguities. There's a question as to how, as human beings, we are able to read pictures in a way that animals can't. In recent years it's been discovered that vision itself is not simply an optical phenomenon. It isn't that your eye acts as a mirror that turns everything upside down and then your mind puts it right side up again, which is what I was told as a kid. In fact, you see only the thing that you are looking directly at, more or less, and everything in the periphery is invented by your mind. It's a live visual activity in combination with a highly sophisticated intellectual one, based on memory; the mind knows how to fill in the bits. When I'm looking at you I'm seeing the room around you too, because my mind has learned how to do it.

It's experience, from knowledge as well as perception.
It's through knowledge that you see. I do a drawing of a shoe and I make the shoe ten feet tall and purple with a green sole. Anybody looking at it knows that it's a shoe, that it's not purple, that it's not green; they know what size it should be, what it's for, what it's made out of, they have an idea of what it costs. None of this is expressed in the image. All of it is what one brings to the object, that's how we understand the world. That's why I never draw anything you can't identify; I don't draw funny plumbing parts. I only give you things you can identify quickly, so you're looking at the thing without speculating.

So, given that most of the paintings for Windsor are new, how did you choose the particular objects for this series? Is there a visual clarity or a certain randomness to this particular moment?
I'm trying to push as many memory buttons as I can. One of the images in the exhibition is an American football, which obviously wouldn't mean as much in England as it does in America. I've got things that touch on music, like a guitar; things to do with contemporary technologies, like a laptop and an iPhone; things to do with contemporary clothing, like trainers. Some people are greatly put off by certain things, which is weird to me, I'm kind of happy with all of them.

I love the idea that things are constantly live, there's a Flux element to that.

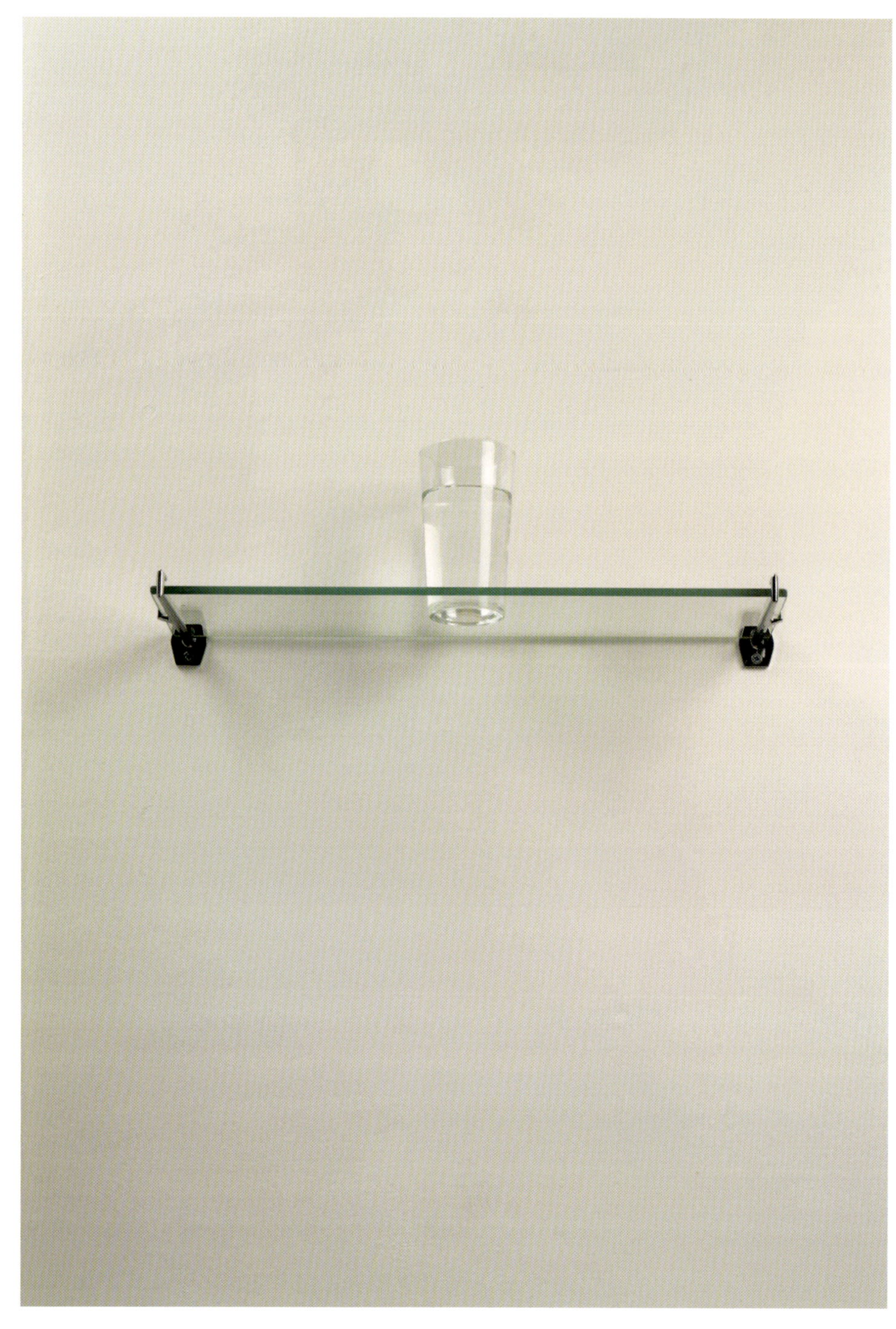

Q: To begin with, could you describe this work?
A: Yes, of course. What I've done is change a glass of water into a full-grown oak tree without altering the accidents of the glass of water.
Q: The accidents?
A: Yes. The colour, feel, weight, size …
Q: Do you mean that the glass of water is a symbol of an oak tree?
A: No. It's not a symbol. I've changed the physical substance of the glass of water into that of an oak tree.
Q: It looks like a glass of water …
A: Of course it does. I didn't change its appearance. But it's not a glass of water. It's an oak tree.
Q: Can you prove what you claim to have done?
A: Well, yes and no. I claim to have maintained the physical form of the glass of water and, as you can see, I have. However, as one normally looks for evidence of physical change in terms of altered form, no such proof exists.
Q: Haven't you simply called this glass of water an oak tree?
A: Absolutely not. It is not a glass of water any more. I have changed its actual substance. It would no longer be accurate to call it a glass of water. One could call it anything one wished but that would not alter the fact that it is an oak tree.
Q: Isn't this just a case of the emperor's new clothes?
A: No. With the emperor's new clothes people claimed to see something which wasn't there because they felt they should. I would be very surprised if anyone told me they saw an oak tree.
Q: Was it difficult to effect the change?
A: No effort at all. But it took me years of work before I realized I could do it.
Q: When precisely did the glass of water become an oak tree?
A: When I put water in the glass.
Q: Does this happen every time you fill a glass with water?
A: No, of course not. Only when I intend to change it into an oak tree.
Q: Then intention causes the change?
A: I would say it precipitates the change.
Q: You don't know how you do it?
A: It contradicts what I feel I know about cause and effect.
Q: It seems to me you're claiming to have worked a miracle. Isn't that the case?
A: I'm flattered that you think so.
Q: But aren't you the only person who can do something like this?
A: How could I know?
Q: Could you teach others to do it?
A: No. It's not something one can teach.
Q: Do you consider that changing the glass of water into an oak tree constitutes an artwork?
A: Yes.
Q: What precisely is the artwork? The glass of water?
A: There is no glass of water any more.
Q: The process of change?
A: There is no process involved in the change.
Q: The oak tree?
A: Yes. the oak tree.
Q: But the oak tree only exists in the mind.
A: No. The actual oak tree is physically present but in the form of the glass of water. As the glass of water was a particular glass of water, the oak tree is also particular. To conceive the category 'oak tree' or to picture a particular oak tree is not to understand and experience what appears to be a glass of water as an oak tree. Just as it is imperceivable, it is also inconceivable.
Q: Did the particular oak tree exist somewhere else before it took the form of the glass of water?
A: No. This particular oak tree did not exist previously. I should also point out that it does not and will not ever have any other form but that of a glass of water.
Q: How long will it continue to be an oak tree?
A: Until I change it.

An Oak Tree, 1973
Assorted objects and printed text, 6 × 18¼ × 5½ in. (15 × 46 × 14 cm)
National Gallery of Australia

I've found over the years I draw as constantly as I can. I sometimes can't find anything to draw for weeks and then suddenly find ten things and one drawing leads me to another, week after week. I might use the drawings if I'm excited because they are new; or I might put them away and only come across them years later. Sometimes I use drawings that I've done thirty years ago. I draw the same way today as I did in 1978; I've gotten better, there are changes, but in general the language of that simple line is exactly the same. It means that these drawings are all live to me, none are in the past or present. The vocabulary just exists and I can dip in and out of it as I please. When I published a book of over 300 drawings [2015], I didn't put them in the chronology in which I did them, partly because I've never paid any attention to it and couldn't accurately do it, but mainly because I don't think of them as having a chronology.

Reductively looking at the selection of images that are going to be shown across the different media at Windsor, I was thinking that Windsor is many things – as well as a community it's also a collection of buildings in an exquisitely manicured landscape next to the ocean. Do the architectural motifs in your work have any relationship to that or is it serendipitous?
I like the idea of a reference to architecture. I'm very interested in architecture and the relation of buildings as objects and objects of design. It seems to me that there are four great architects of the twentieth century who have defined what the modern world looks like: Frank Lloyd Wright, Mies van der Rohe, Corbusier and Rietveld. Each designed both furniture and architecture, so I've taken one piece of furniture and one of their buildings and put them together in a set of four prints called *Design and Architecture* [2017]. I always do the prints in series, because there's a dialogue that you can create in a series. I can't do that in paintings.

And your sculptures will frame, and be framed, by buildings as well as the landscape. You've hinted that you've made a trail around them.
Yes, it was very interesting to do the trail. A key place is the edge of a lake, on the golf course, where there are two *Umbrellas*; in general, the sculptures are singular, but having two here creates a particular tension between the images and the landscape. It's the kind of place where you might get caught in a storm and you'd be grateful to have an umbrella, it's very open. There's a sense that with a gust of wind, the umbrellas would be in the lake, whereas *Garden Fork* is in a closed garden, sitting on a small patch of ground. A fork is an object that could make sense there.

There's a logic but also, because of the scale and colour, a sense of absurdity.
I'm not po-faced, I'm not trying to teach anybody anything. I'm playing in an area between design and art. I increasingly think that art is essentially

about observation; artists notice things and draw your attention to
what is already there, which you haven't noticed because you weren't
focusing. The realm of invention is that of designers; they invent new
chairs, new technologies. I'm trying to say something about these
objects but I don't invent them, I just look at them.

**But you subtly transform by reduction and by the addition of colour,
and context of course is critical. I've seen _Garden Fork_ at Chatsworth
in front of a grand neoclassical façade [2014]. I've seen _Garden Fork_ in
Hong Kong vying for our attention with the harbour [2017]. The objects
are constant but they shift our perception of what's around and our
perception of them shifts.**
The only other time I've shown a large group of sculptures was at
Chatsworth and that is such a particular setting. There's a significant
difference between the climate, vegetation and light in the North of
England and in Florida. The sculptures will come alive in a different way.
I'm curious. I've always said that the only reason for making things as
an artist is out of curiosity to see them.

**You did a beautiful sculptural installation in front of the Peninsula
Hotel in Hong Kong [_Bright Idea_, 2016]. A yellow light bulb looked at
first as if it were emerging out of the water, but then as if it were
balancing improbably on top of a small bush. Your attention was acute
as to how it would be sited but it was still surprising for you to see
the sculpture when it was installed.**
I will have an idea that makes me do the thing in the first place. Then
the thing exists and it has another idea – not necessarily the one that
I started with, sometimes better. Essentially artworks need to try to
capture the eye, and the imagination, of the viewer. And if you can
do that, it allows some speculative room for the viewer. That's really
something very special.

I look forward to seeing the results at Windsor, as do you I suppose.
I absolutely do.

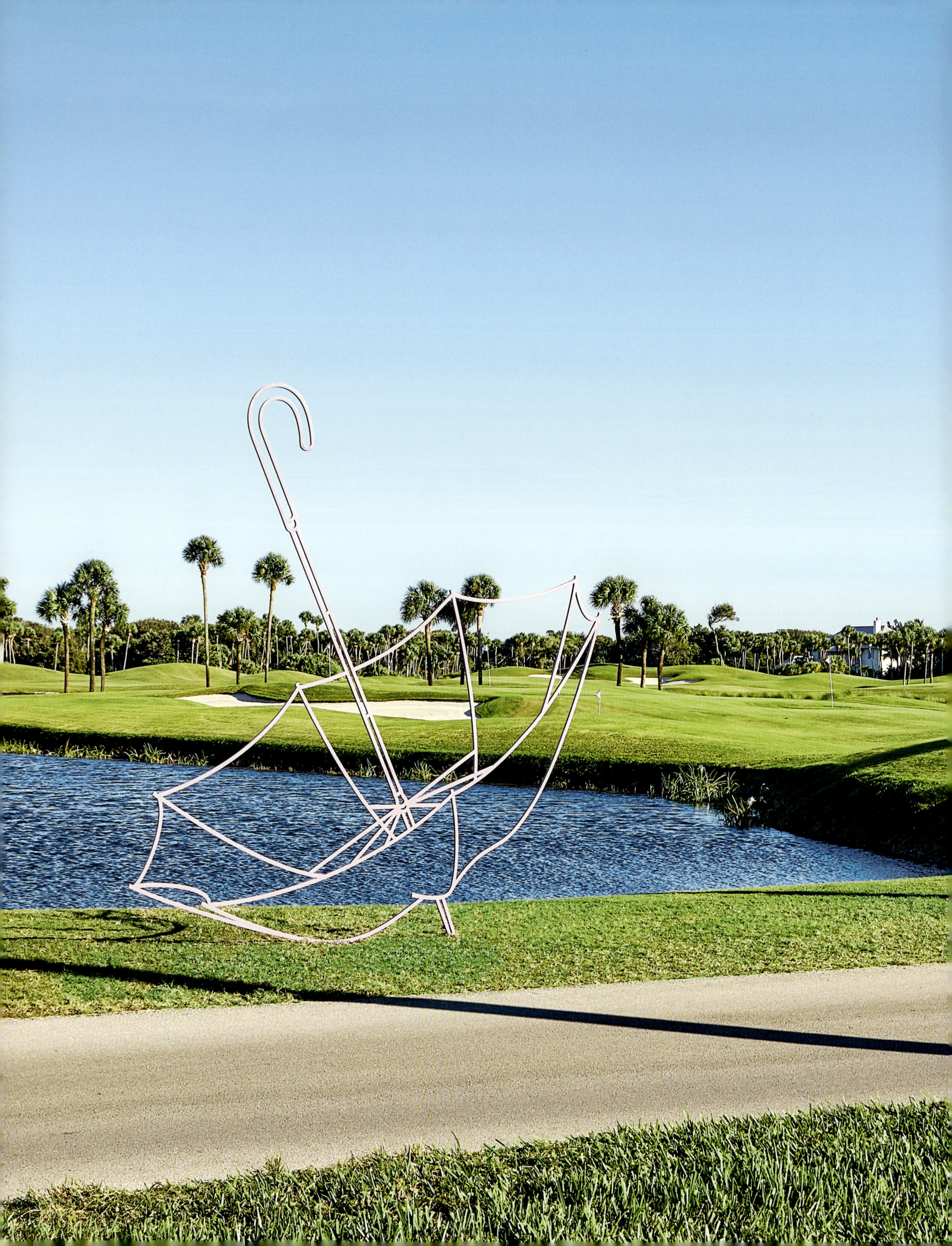

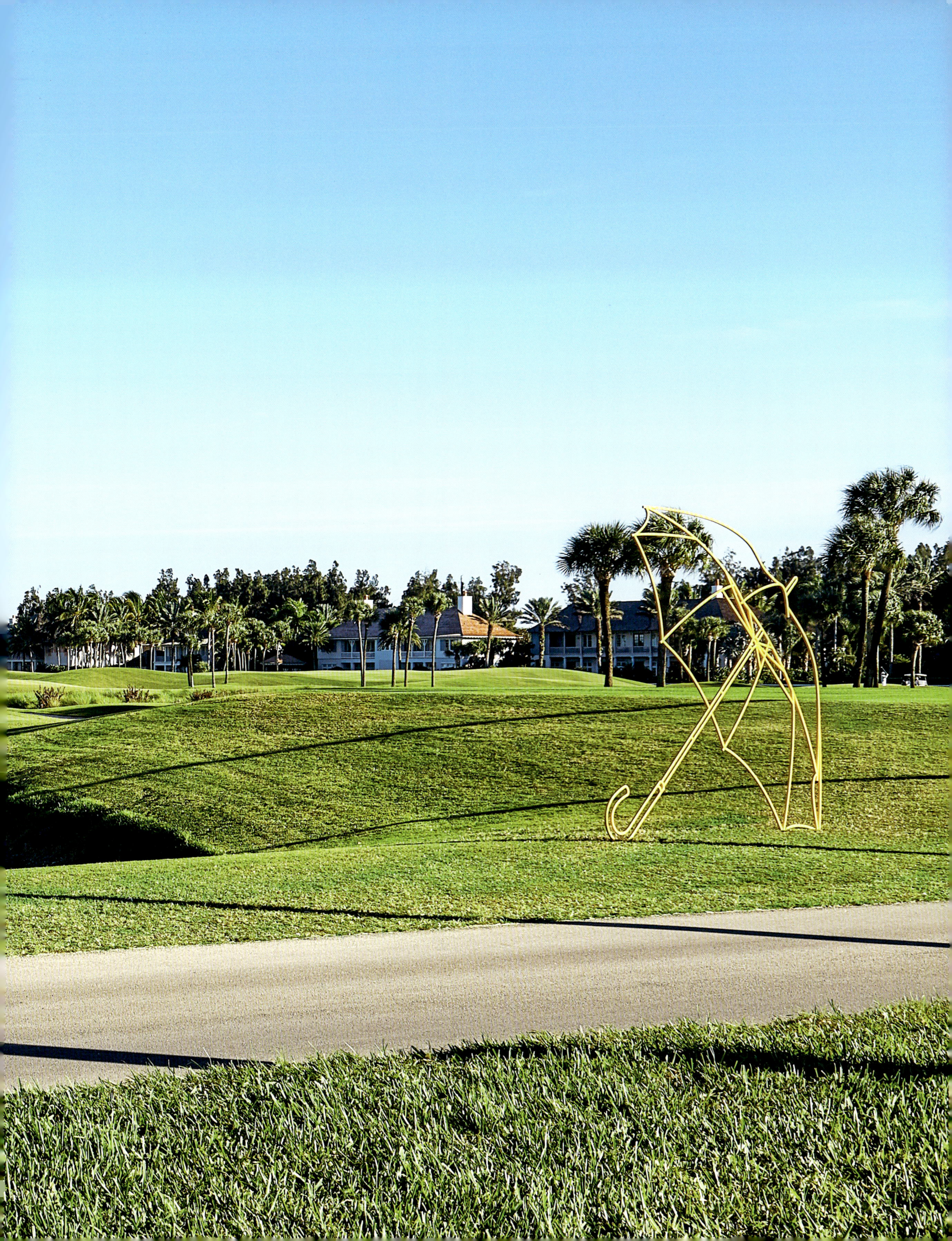

Josef Albers
Homage to the Square, 1963
Oil on masonite, 40 × 40 in. (101.6 × 101.6 cm)
Museum of Fine Arts, Houston, Texas, USA
Gift of Anni Albers and the Josef Albers Foundation, Inc.

Art in the Present Sense

Ben Luke is an art critic at the London *Evening Standard*, and features editor and podcast host at *The Art Newspaper*. He has written essays about and interviewed many leading international artists. He is a member of the advisory board of the Government Art Collection, UK.

1 Interview with the author, 24 August 2018. Unless otherwise stated, all quotes from Michael Craig-Martin are from this interview.
2 Email to the author, 17 October 2018.

On walking into Michael Craig-Martin's East London studio, you are overwhelmed by colour. Accidental swatches of paint punctuate the white walls – ghostly traces of the process, where colour has spilled over the edge of the surface. A patchwork of encrusted spatters decorates a huge sink in the middle of the room. Bottles of acrylics are gathered in orderly groups on the floor. And, of course, colour bursts from the paintings, the latest that Craig-Martin has made in a now six-decade-long career. The breadth of hues and tones is dizzying: magenta and shocking pink; vermillion red; deep purple; light blue and ultramarine; acid yellow; turquoise and emerald. Contained within the pictures are ordinary objects – an iPhone, a football, a credit card, a sneaker, sunglasses, a light bulb, a laptop – but the effect is anything but ordinary. *Untitled (wireless)* (2018; p.29), for instance, depicts over-ear headphones, a familiar sight in everyday life, and yet here, on a vast scale at two and a half metres high, set against candy pink, with turquoise and purple ear pads and a sky-blue headband, they have an almost psychedelic, otherworldly presence. Within Craig-Martin's paintings is a world of vivid sensation, of unexpected pleasures, that belies the prosaic nature of the items he depicts. It is this ability to make the routine strange, to imbue the quotidian with deep sensory and emotional resonance, that makes Craig-Martin such a compelling artist.

New work builds on a specific pictorial language that Craig-Martin has developed since the mid-1970s, but which derives from his experiences as a student at Yale University between 1961 and 1966. It was a profound period of learning for Craig-Martin, both formally and informally. Yale was the most influential art school in America, producing major artists such as Richard Serra, Chuck Close, Nancy Graves and Brice Marden. As master's students, some objected to the courses in Basic Drawing, Basic Design, Basic Sculpture and Color – a legacy of the Bauhaus artist Josef Albers, who taught at Yale during the 1950s. Craig-Martin, however, fully embraced his teachings. He recognises today that, regarding colour, 'everything I do is based on what I learned from Albers, everything.'[1]

The most obvious example in his present exhibition at The Gallery at Windsor are the *Double Take* paintings, based on an exercise from Albers's colour course. Here Craig-Martin is attempting 'to play with the realisation that the choice of colour can be simultaneously arbitrary and critical by just reversing the ground colour with the principal image colour'.[2] In *Double Take (iPhone)* (2018; pp.38–39), Craig-Martin has placed an image of an iPhone at the centre of two 90 cm square panels; on the left, the ground is turquoise and the trim around the edge of the iPhone is his characteristic magenta; on the right, the colours are reversed. Meanwhile the screen is sky blue in each image. The spatial effect is markedly different: amid the turquoise, the iPhone pulls up to the surface; amid the pink it retreats. The screen, though exactly the same blue in both panels, seems infinitely cooler and darker surrounded by turquoise. On the one hand, this is a spirited homage to Albers, riffing on his academic exercises. But on the other, Craig-Martin lifts a colour exercise from theory into public experience, and emphasises that colour perception is a fundamental part of seeing the world.

Just as important in his development as an artist in the 1960s, were his experiences of discovering contemporary art in New York. His time at Yale was bookended by the emergence of Pop art and Minimalism. In New York, he saw shows by Jasper Johns, Robert Rauschenberg and several by Andy Warhol. In 1965, he first saw the work of the Minimalists, later writing that it changed the way that he looked at the world.[3] 'In terms of my development, the impact of seeing all of those things has never left me', he says today. In his paintings of the last thirty years and in recent sculptures, Craig-Martin has pushed forward the concerns of those 1960s American movements. He has taken a language of image-making and a saturated colour sense from Pop and allied it to the frankness, directness and physicality he so admires in Minimalism.

Craig-Martin had almost immediate success after moving from the US to the UK in 1966. He developed challenging but playful work, clearly influenced by Minimalism but also building on the entertaining enquiries into art, perception and representation of Marcel Duchamp, whose use of found objects he adopted. This culminated in Craig-Martin's most celebrated early conceptual piece, *An Oak Tree* (1973; pp.14–15). It features a glass of water on a shelf, accompanied by an interview between an artist and a sceptic about the artist's contention that he has turned the glass of water into an oak tree. *An Oak Tree* has been shown so broadly that the text has been translated into forty languages.

Following this, Craig-Martin turned from using real objects to drawing them, much as he had been taught at Yale, where Albers had compared learning to draw with practising the violin. He realised that by making images of an object he was not 'using it up' as he was with the found objects. Images can be detached from their context, expanded, reduced, combined with other things: they are reusable. He initially sought to find readymade drawings of readymade objects, but to his surprise discovered that none existed – so he began creating them himself. The impersonal character of the drawings echoes Duchamp's process of choosing a readymade 'neither by its beauty nor by its ugliness. To find a point of indifference in my looking at it.'[4]

Craig-Martin found indifference in the most ordinary of objects. He had long admired Warhol's approach of only depicting things that were famous: Hollywood stars, consumer products, even the electric chair. But the ordinary, as Craig-Martin says, is 'more famous than famous. So famous you don't even notice.' He has taken Jasper Johns's idea of depicting 'things the mind already knows' to an extreme.

The Windsor exhibition is testament to this intention. Craig-Martin makes images in outline – the viewer can instantly name the object and its

3 Michael Craig-Martin, *On Being an Artist*, Art/Books, London, 2015, p.84.
4 Marcel Duchamp, interview with Joan Bakewell, *Late Night Line-Up*, BBC2, June 1968, https://www.bbc.co.uk/programmes/p04826th, accessed 15 May 2018.

purpose, understand the materials it was made from, know how it feels to touch and use it. And yet none of that information is in the image. Take *Untitled (lightbulb blue)* (2017; p.33): despite the incongruity of a blue bulb and a green base, the viewer immediately recognises the former as glass and the latter as metal. Recently, Craig-Martin has pushed this further, by depicting fragments of objects. With these details, 'you can still build this entire sense of the thing beyond the scope of what you can see', he says. In *Untitled (trainer fragment)* (2017; p.55), from a close-up of the tongue of the shoe, its laces and hints of other design details, you can conjure the entire object, detect the Adidas brand, imagine its tactile qualities and perhaps even what it feels like to wear it.

To aid the neutrality of his language, Craig-Martin originally made outline drawings in pencil and then traced them using fine drawing tape onto acetate. He aimed to make 'a styleless language of drawing'. Yet, paradoxically, it has become a recognisable style, inimitably Craig-Martin, especially since the drawings were allied to colour in earnest in the early 1990s. Given its centrality to his work today, it is remarkable that he once had an avowed fear of colour. He had experimented for years, initially working only with the primaries, with the same pursuit of detachment he adopted in his approach to drawing: red, yellow and blue being the ABC of colour, sharing the objects' ordinariness. But it was when he opened up his palette that Craig-Martin's work truly evolved. Colour, he found, could still feel readymade with a palette of twelve rather than three.

Craig-Martin's choice of colour reinforces the sense of immediacy, like an electric shock sparking a connection between artist and viewer. But there are distinct subtleties in tones and hues, which explore the viewer's perception of the object. In *Untitled (guitar)* (2018; p.57), he uses black both for the guitar's 'sound hole' and for the 'pick guard' below it, testing our understanding of void and solidity, and the physicality of what is depicted. *Untitled (stiletto)* (2018; p.37) could possibly be an accurate depiction of a green high-heel, or alternatively, an outlandishly coloured image of a much more modest object.

Craig-Martin also knowingly plays with format and language. In *Eye Test* (2018; p.63), he alludes to the light box charts found in opticians and hospitals around the world. Yet he has replaced the letters of the alphabet with his own lexicon of imagery, as immediately recognisable as the ABC. It is a mini 'manifesto' of his art. Craig-Martin also tests our ability to read his images. In *Untitled (split-level)* (2018; pp.60–61), he depicts a particular kind of American vernacular housing, yet by bisecting the split-level structure with differently coloured backgrounds, he emphasises its structural division. The part of the building on the left has blue windows while on the right they are black. He stretches the image's capacity for illusion: the left-hand side feels more three-dimensional because the colour evokes a reflected sky; the black-windowed part on the right feels more diagrammatic.

These latest paintings show how Craig-Martin expands his drawing into a hugely rich and enormously complex body of work. Perhaps the most surprising is in the inexorable intrusion of narrative, which Craig-Martin initially sought to avoid. His work has become a record of time's effect on the objects, and often their progression from use to obsolescence. The very nature of the ordinary has changed: where it once denoted relatively inexpensive things, now highly sophisticated technology is commonplace – a reality to which *Double Take (iPhone)* and *Untitled (laptop magenta)* (2018; p.52) attest. In his series of prints, *Then and Now* (2017; pp.25, 66–67), Craig-Martin documents such shifts in the nature of objects, fusing drawings of older technologies in pale red and their usurpers in black: a boxy television set with a flat, elegant plasma screen; a filing cabinet with a memory stick. One image captures an even more dramatic change, from actual physicality to an absence of object: a cassette overlaid with the Spotify logo.

Another major development is his sculpture. By using supports hidden under the earth, Craig-Martin found a way to make his flat drawings stand up, to be presented outdoors on a grand scale. With no visible plinth, they seem like holograms, monumental yet immaterial; as you walk around them, you see that from the side they are just a single line of painted steel with very little depth. Craig-Martin's sculptures may be read as drawings or paintings.

Installed in the grounds of the Windsor estate, some objects allude to those you might expect to find in a rural setting, like a gardening fork pitched into the ground of a small garden, a white picket gate near the property entrance, or a bright red wheelbarrow near the stables and polo field, but their scale, colour and linear form disrupts any sense of illusion. Viewed outside the context of the gallery, other objects work through sheer incongruity, even surreality: a more than three-metre-wide pink stiletto is found in a residential square, and a pair of similarly giant umbrellas are positioned as though blown by the wind towards a lake beside the golf course.

Throughout his work, Craig-Martin seeks an immediate connection with his audience. Traditionally, he argues, pictures were created to allow the viewer to witness something – a landscape, a person – that the artist has seen and then transformed. However, Craig-Martin does not seek to share a distant experience; like Duchamp, he invites viewers to take a creative role in his art. Their ingrained knowledge of the objects he depicts is crucial to the work's success. This reinforces the fact that it is, as he puts it, 'about the present moment'; Craig-Martin makes art in the present sense.

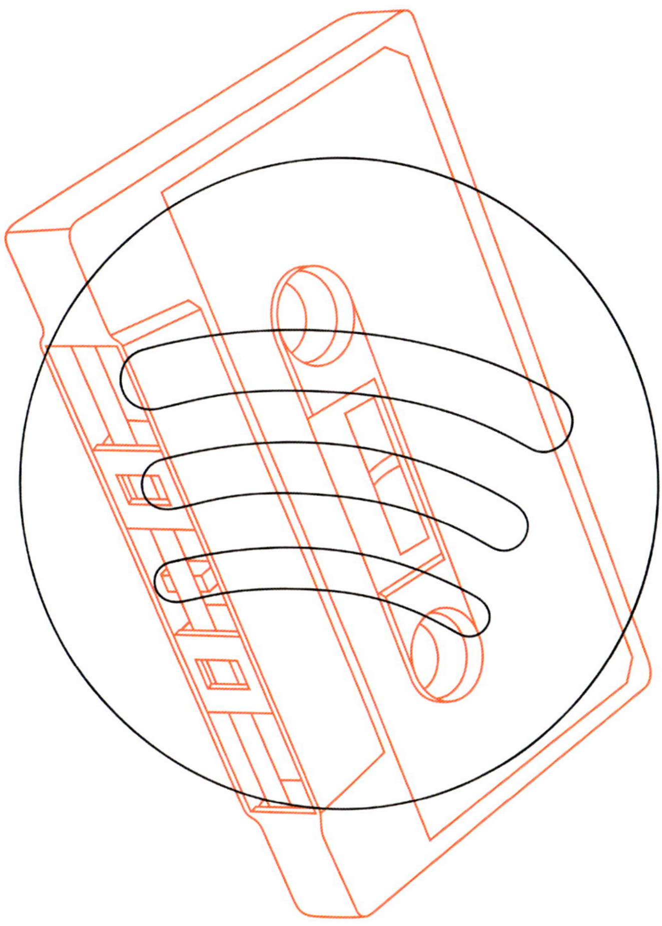

Then and Now (Cassette/Spotify), 2018

Plates

Untitled (wireless), 2018
Acrylic on aluminium, 98½ × 78¾ in. (250 × 200 cm)

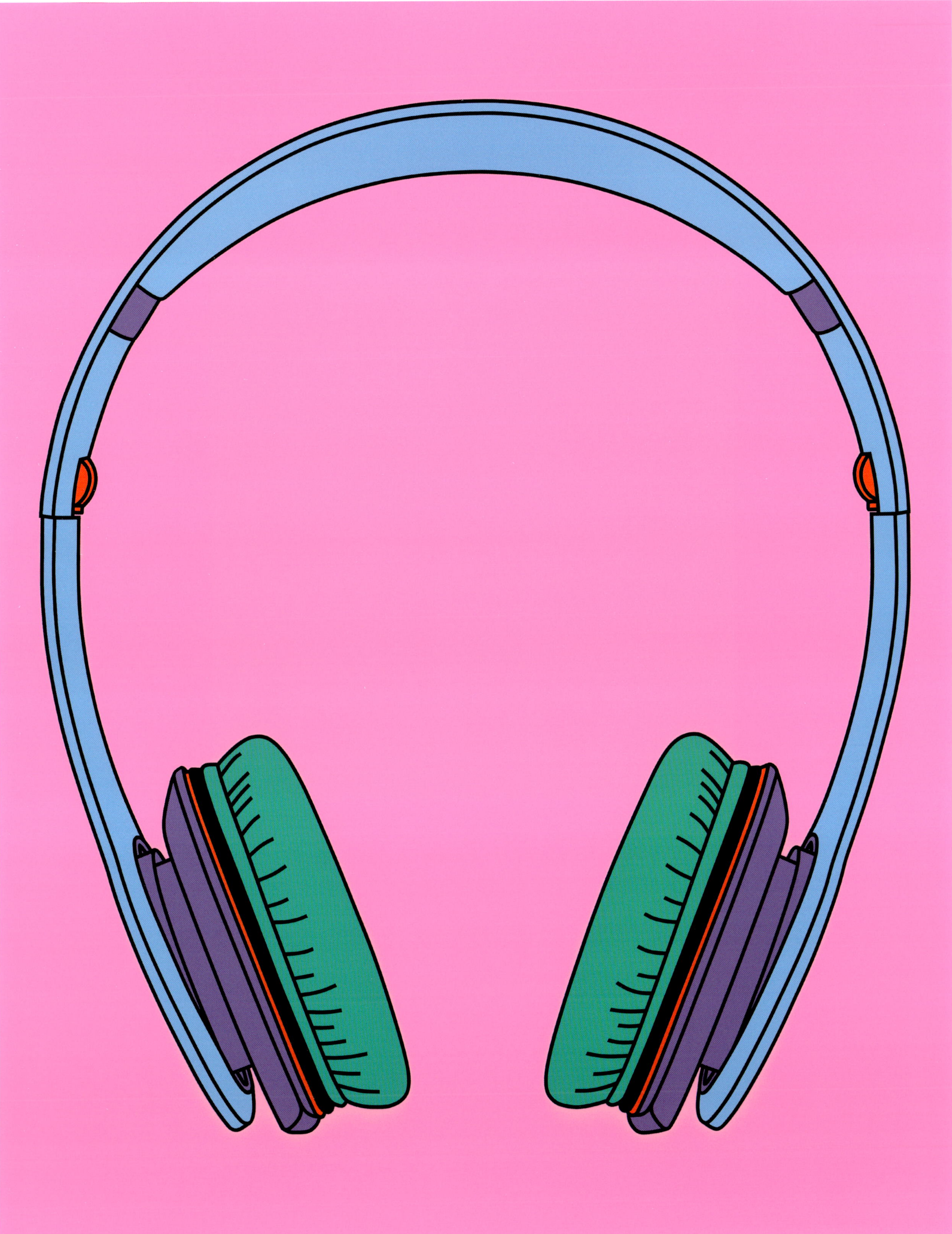

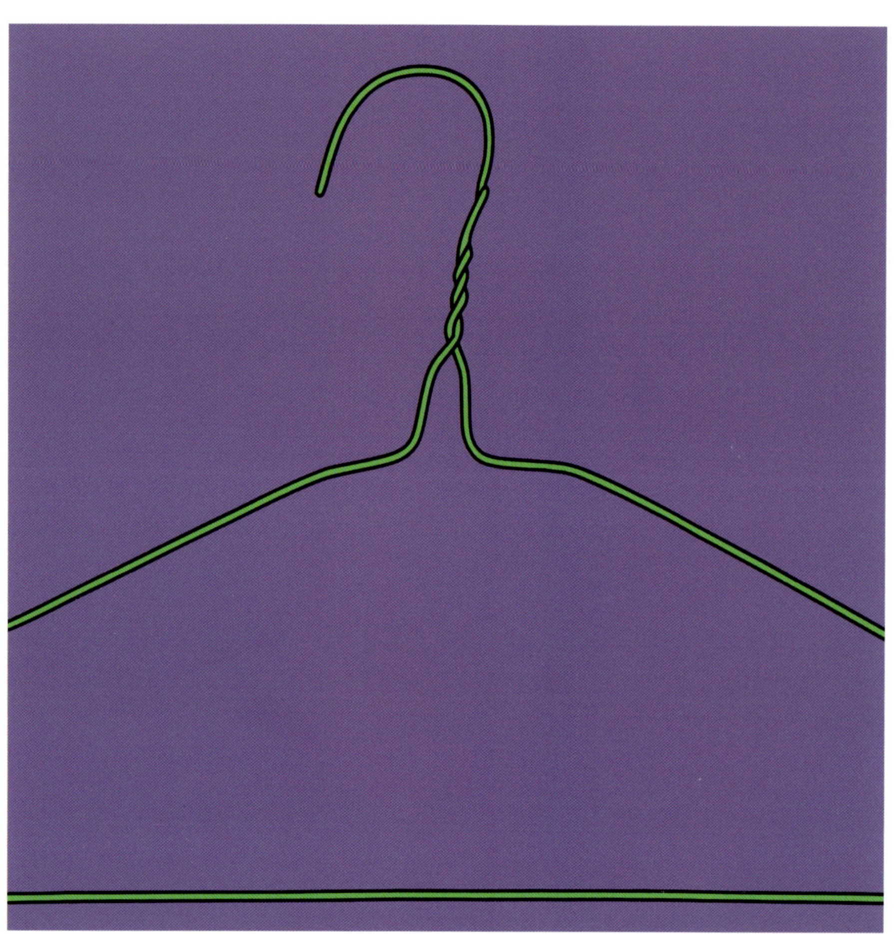

Untitled (coat hanger fragment), 2018
Acrylic on aluminium, 24 × 24 in. (60 × 60 cm)

Untitled (lightbulb blue), 2018
Acrylic on aluminium, 35½ × 35½ in. (90 × 90 cm)

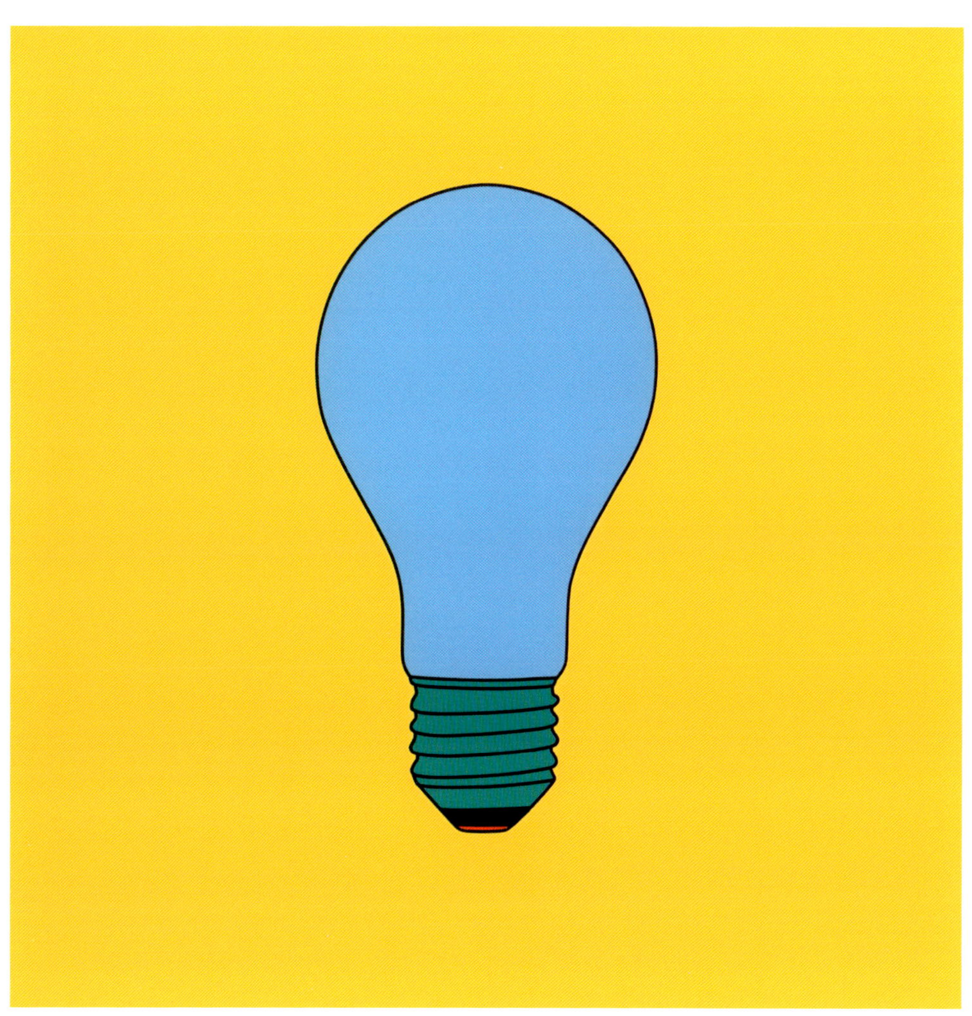

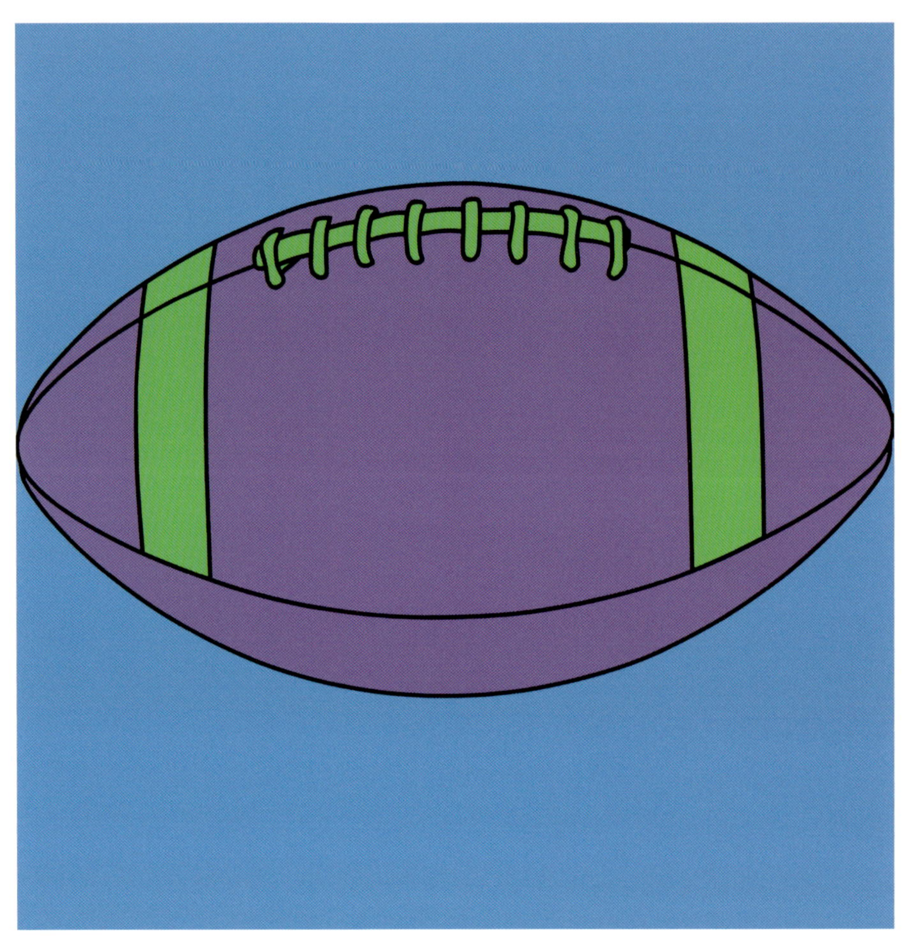

Untitled (American football), 2018
Acrylic on aluminium, 24 × 24 in. (60 × 60 cm)

Untitled (stiletto), 2018
Acrylic on aluminium, 48 × 48 in. (122 × 122 cm)

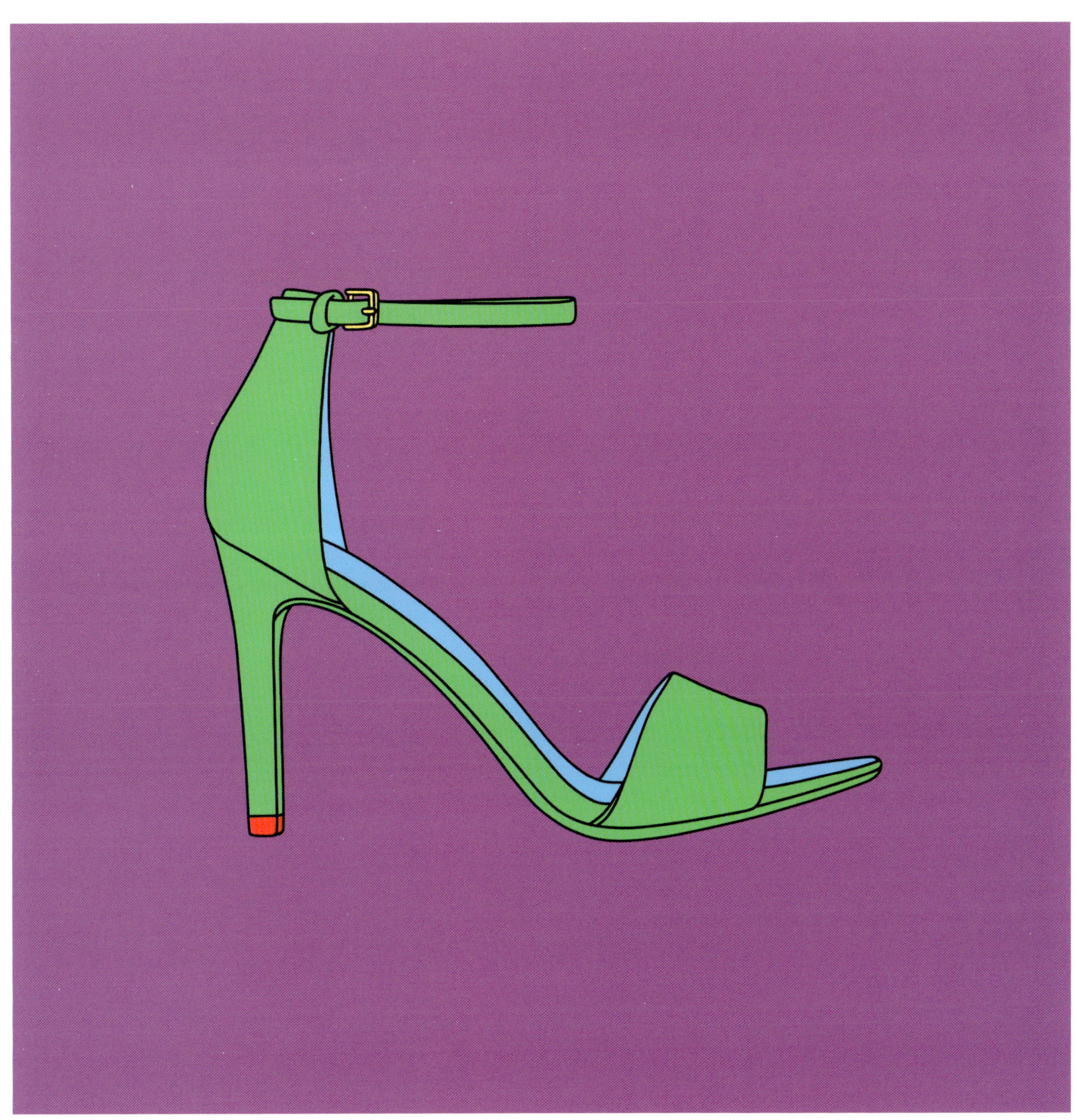

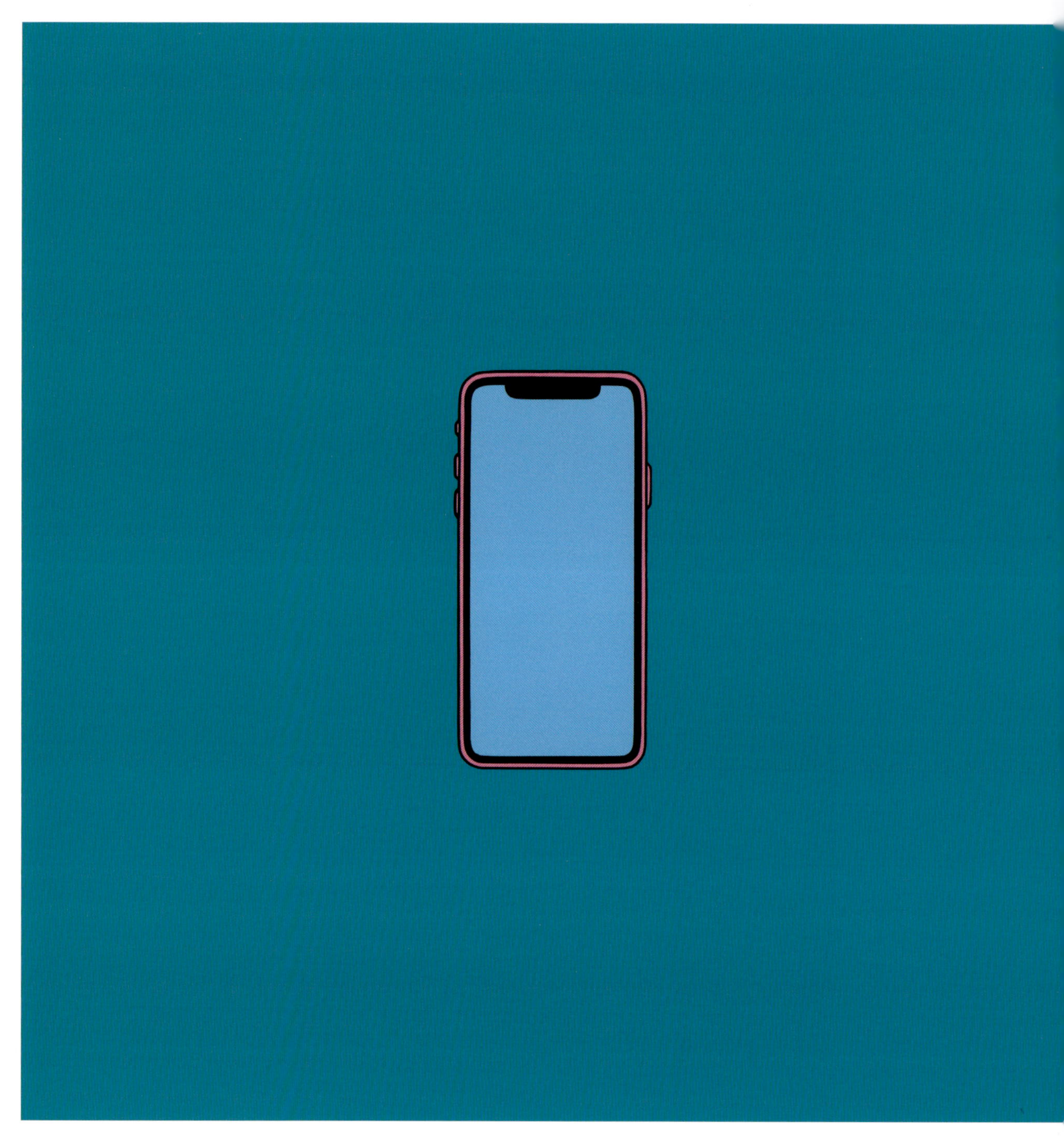

Double Take (iPhone), 2018
Acrylic on aluminium, in two panels, 35½ × 71 in. (90 × 180 cm)

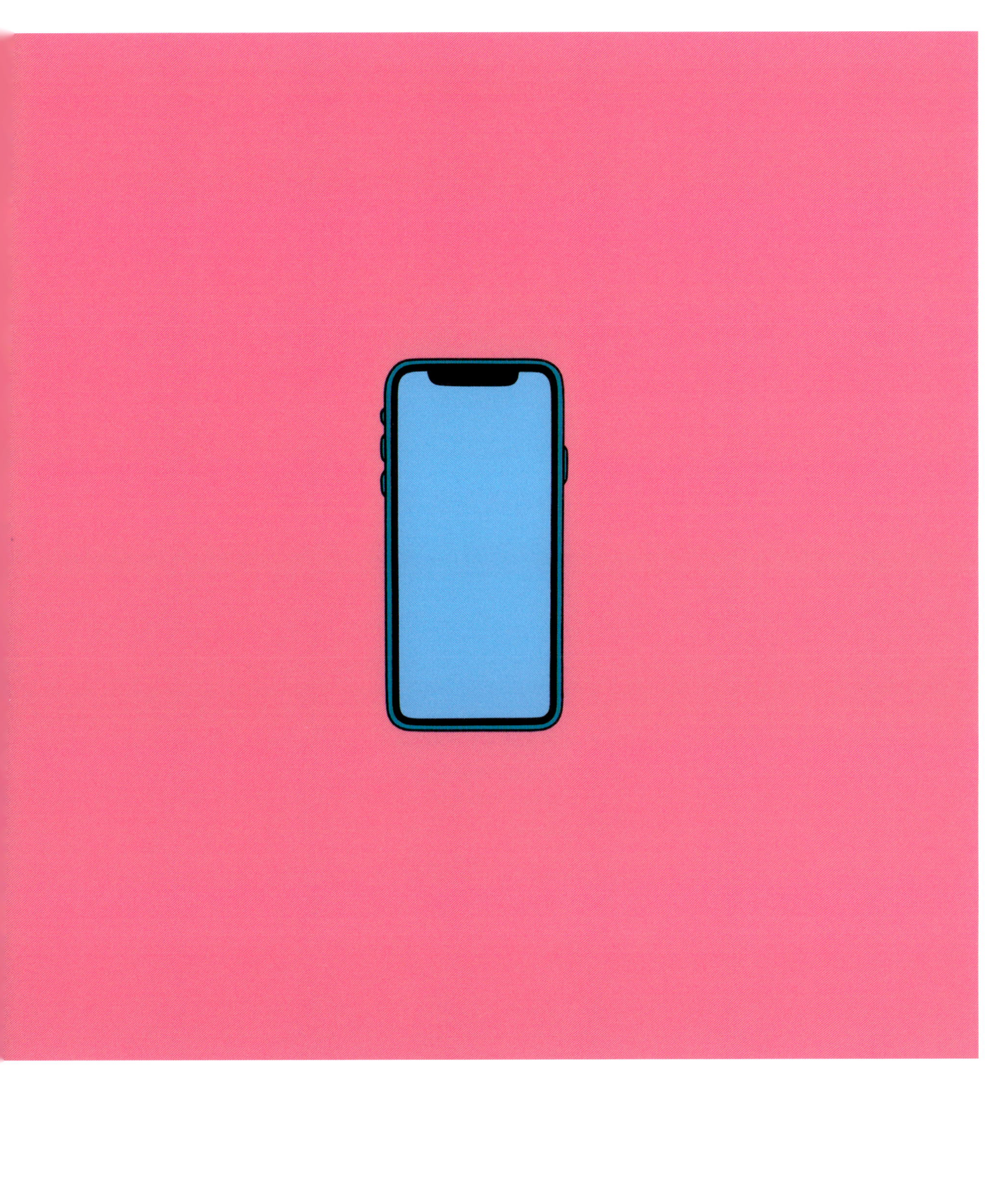

Untitled (sunglasses), 2018
Acrylic on aluminium, 48 × 48 in. (122 × 122 cm)

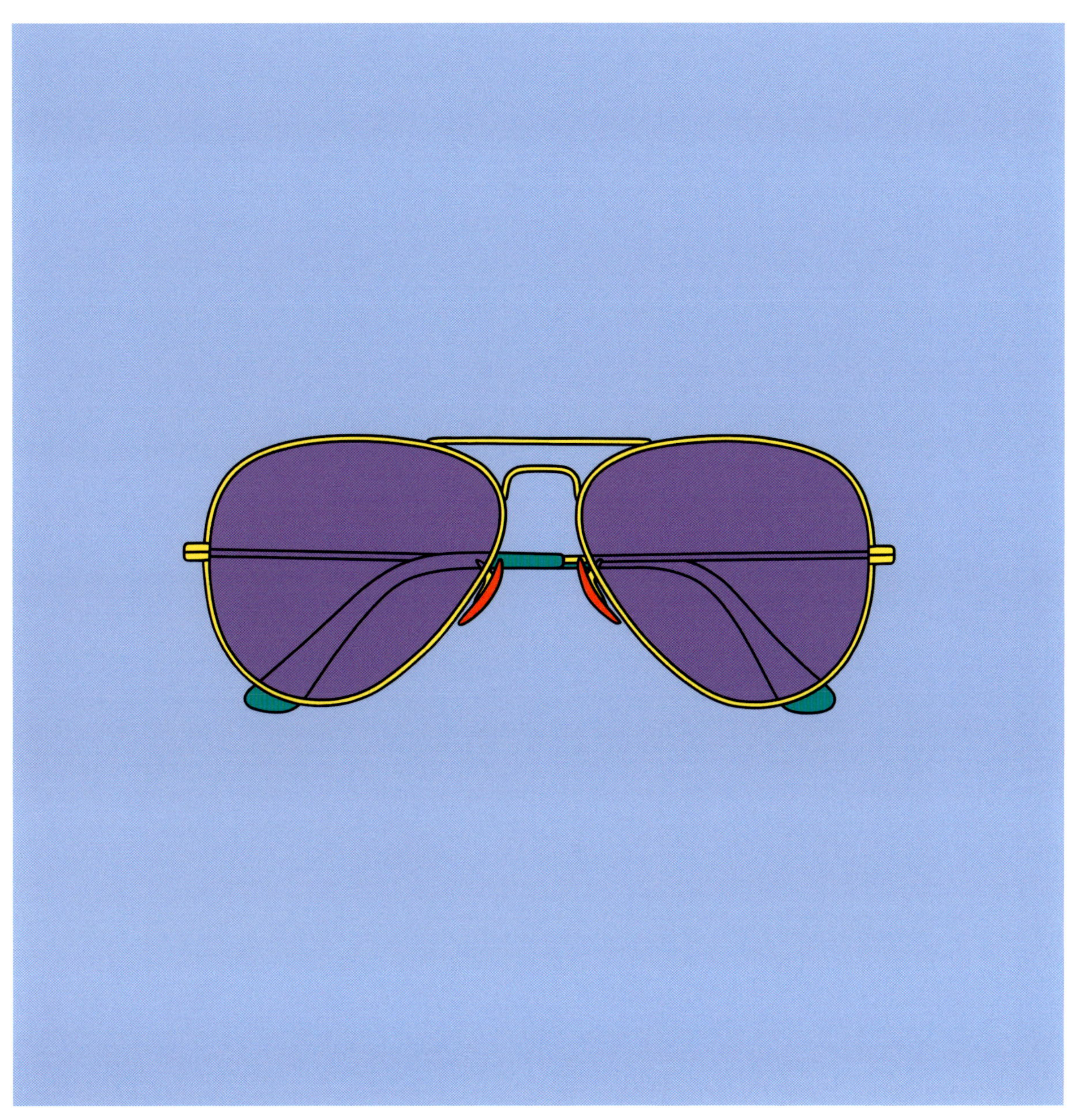

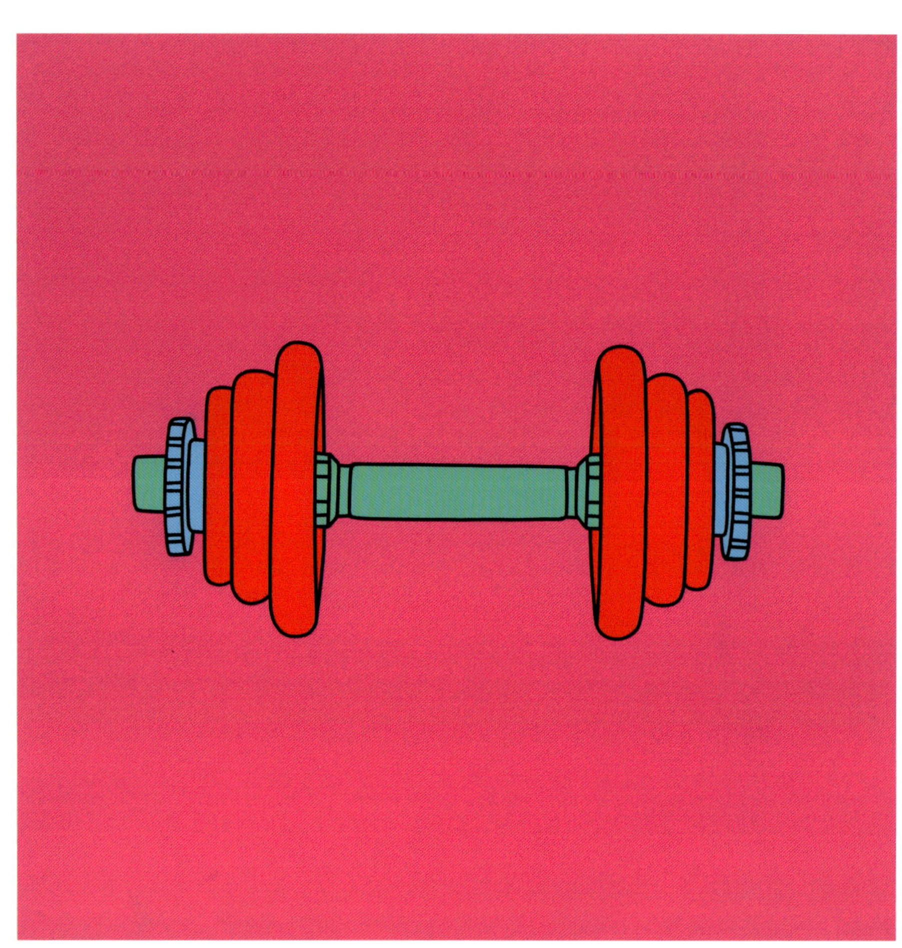

Untitled (dumbbell), 2018
Acrylic on aluminium, 23½ × 23½ in. (60 × 60 cm)

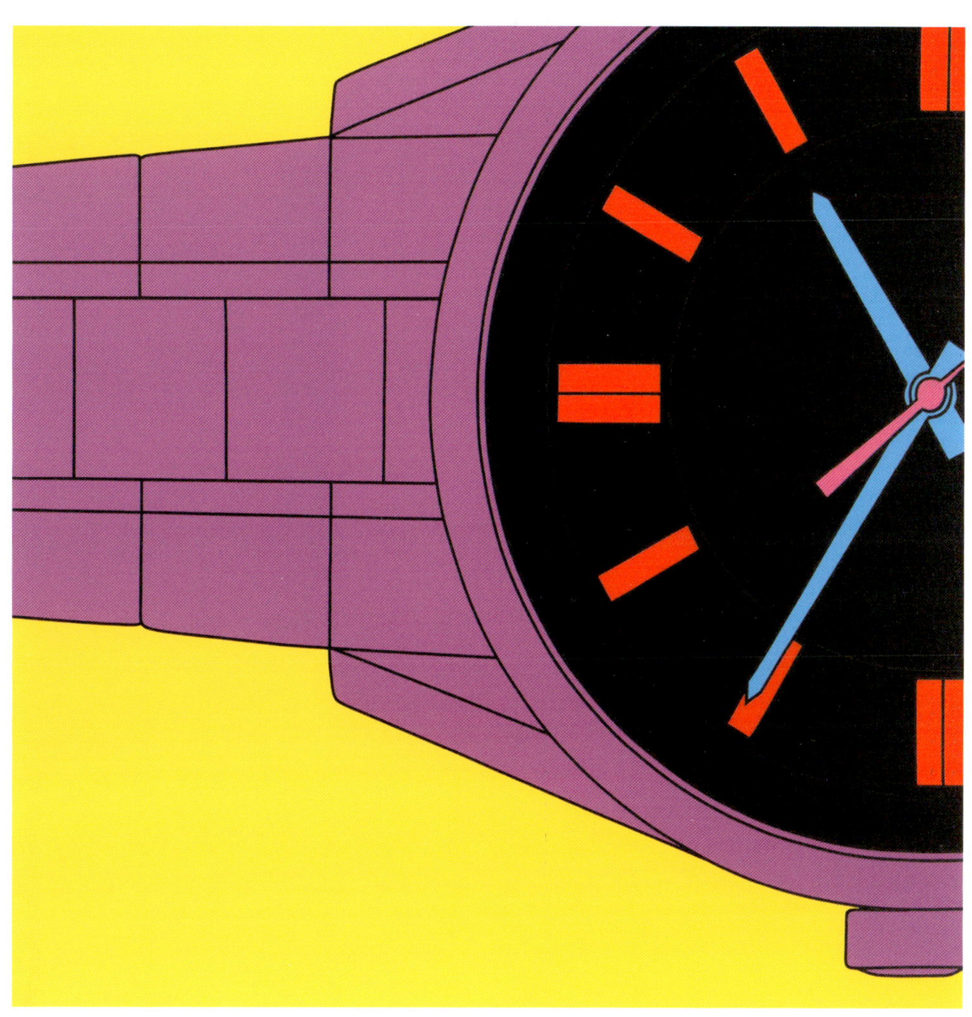

Untitled (corkscrew fragment), 2018
Acrylic on aluminium, 24 × 24 in. (60 × 60 cm)

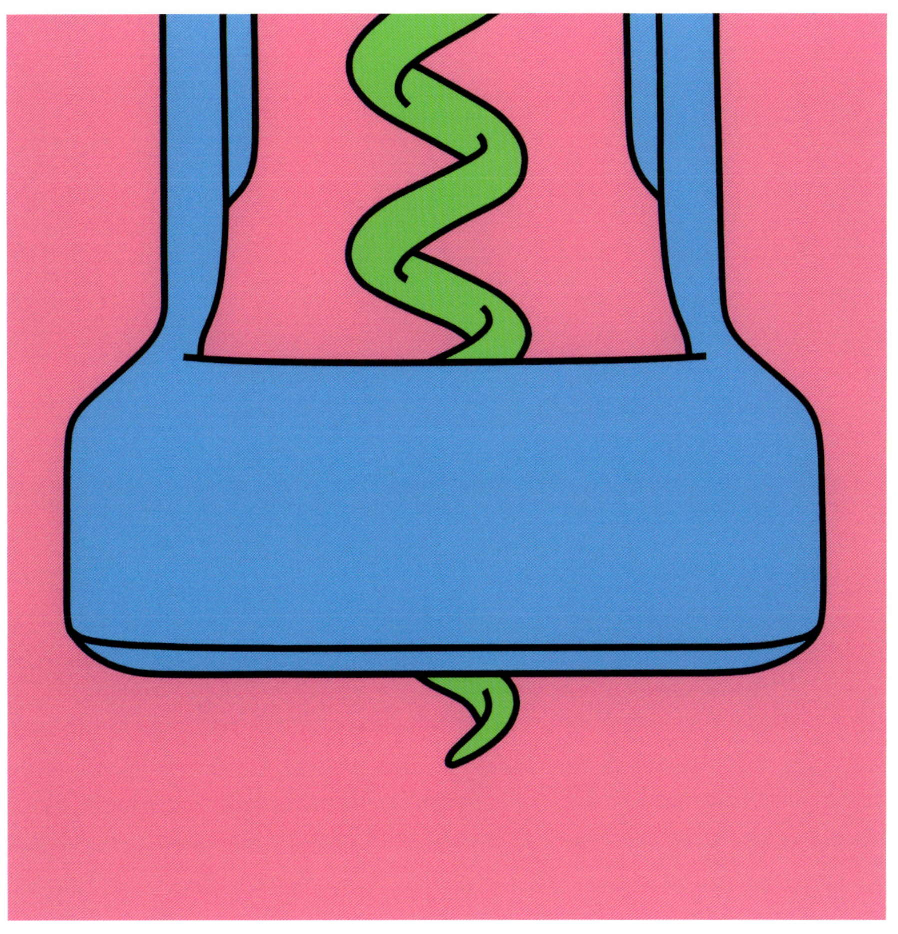

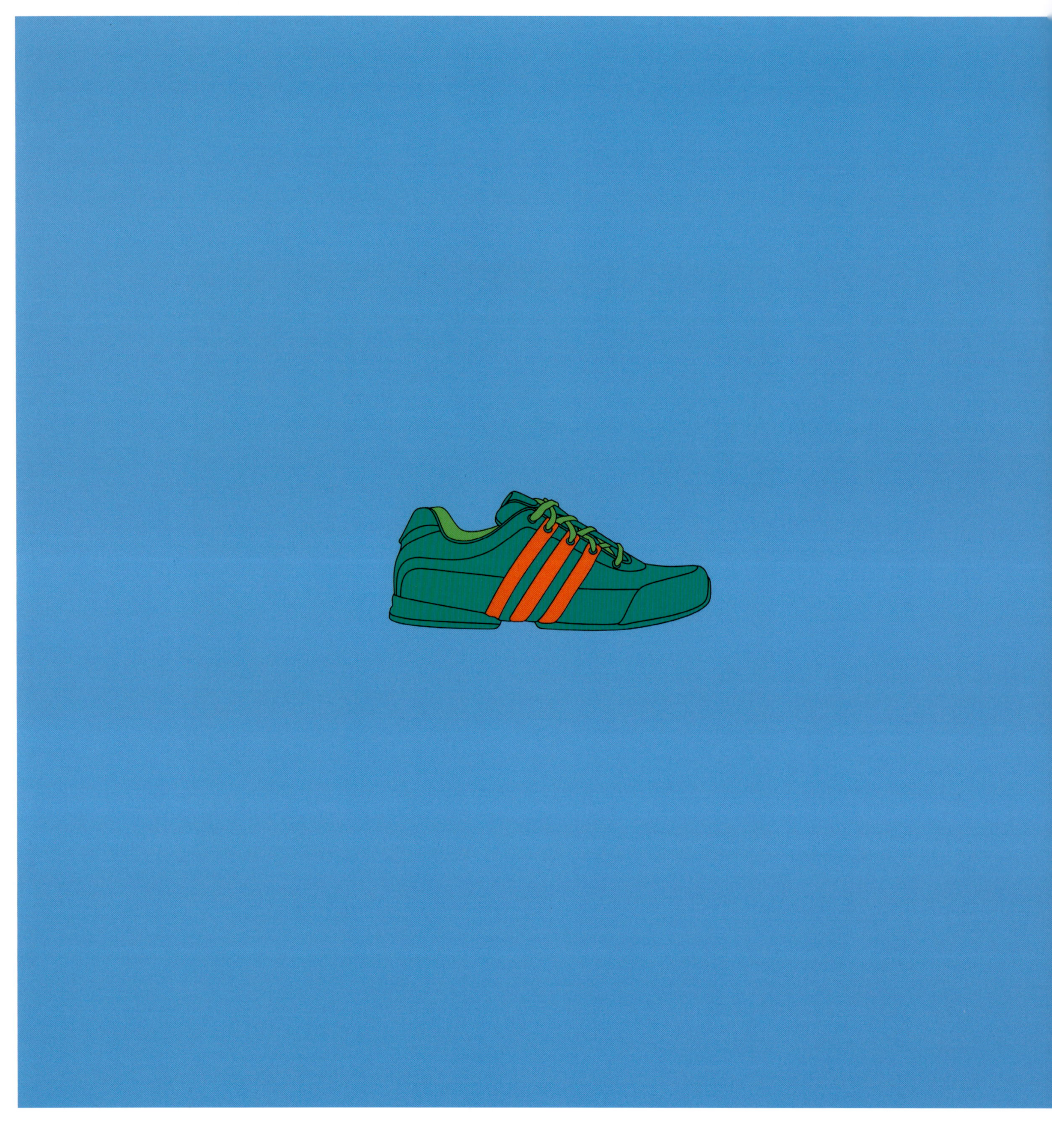

Double Take (trainer), 2018
Acrylic on aluminium, in two panels, 78¾ × 157½ in. (200 × 400 cm)

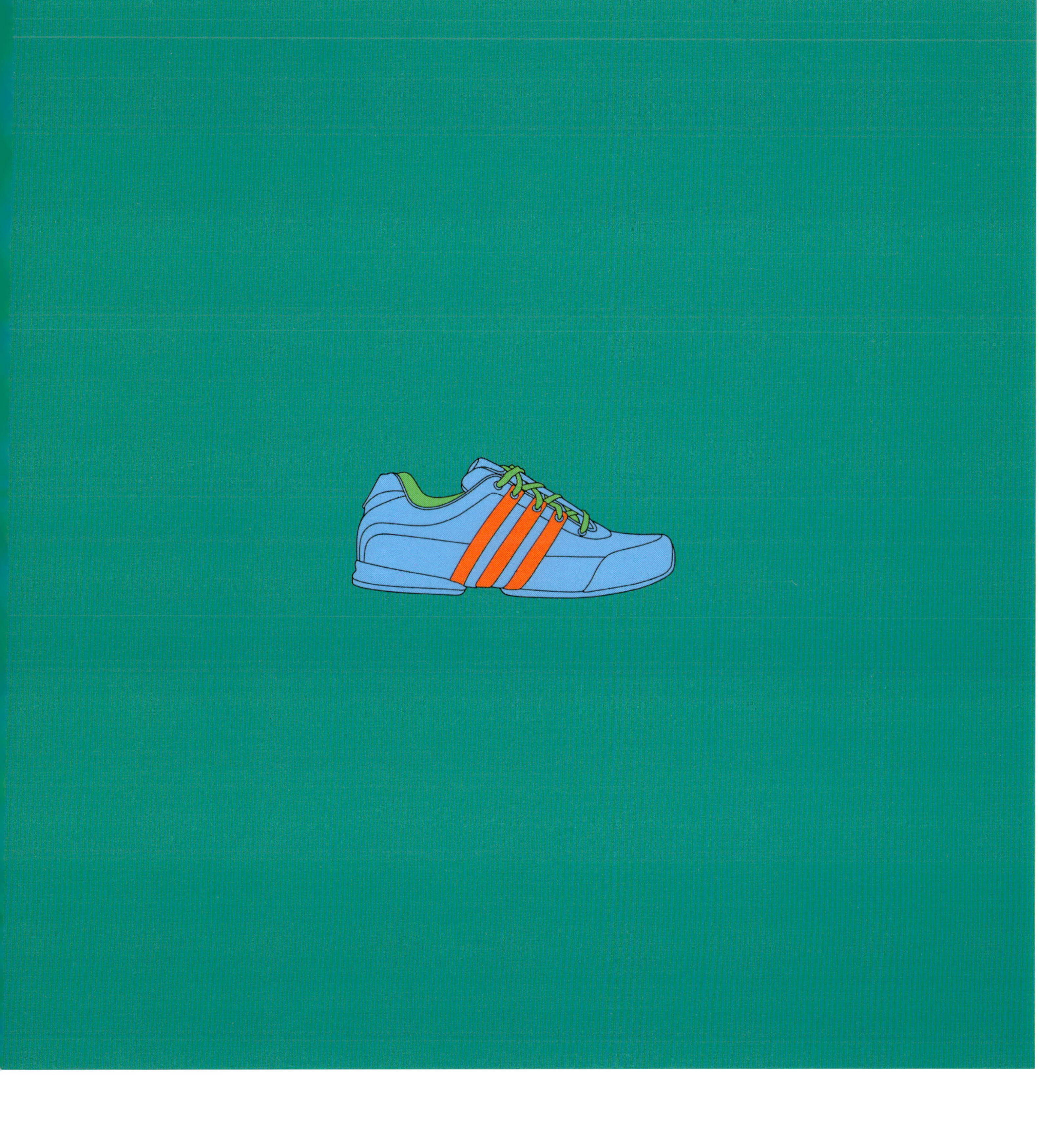

Untitled (credit card), 2014
Acrylic on aluminium, 48 × 48 in. (122 × 122 cm)

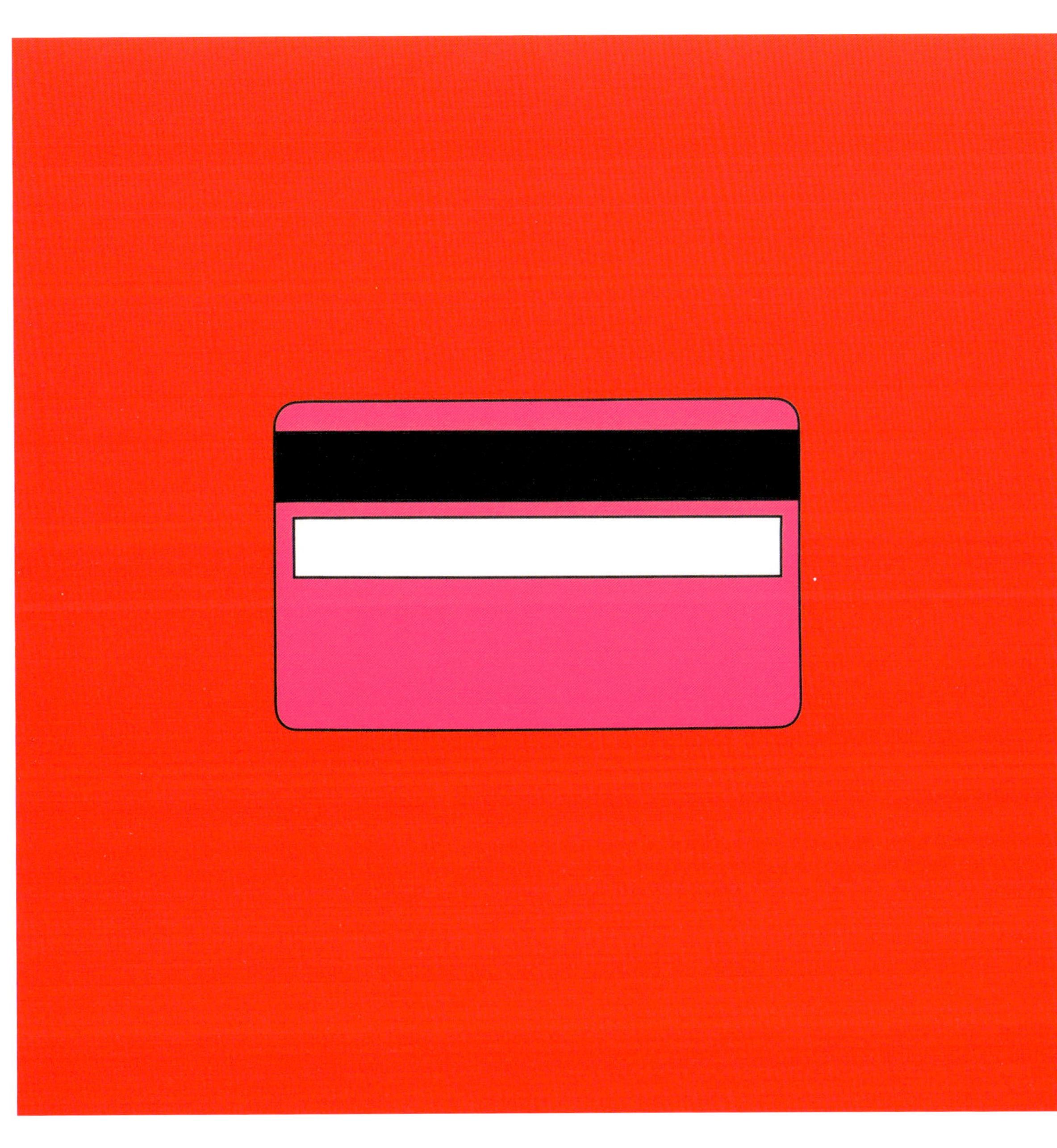

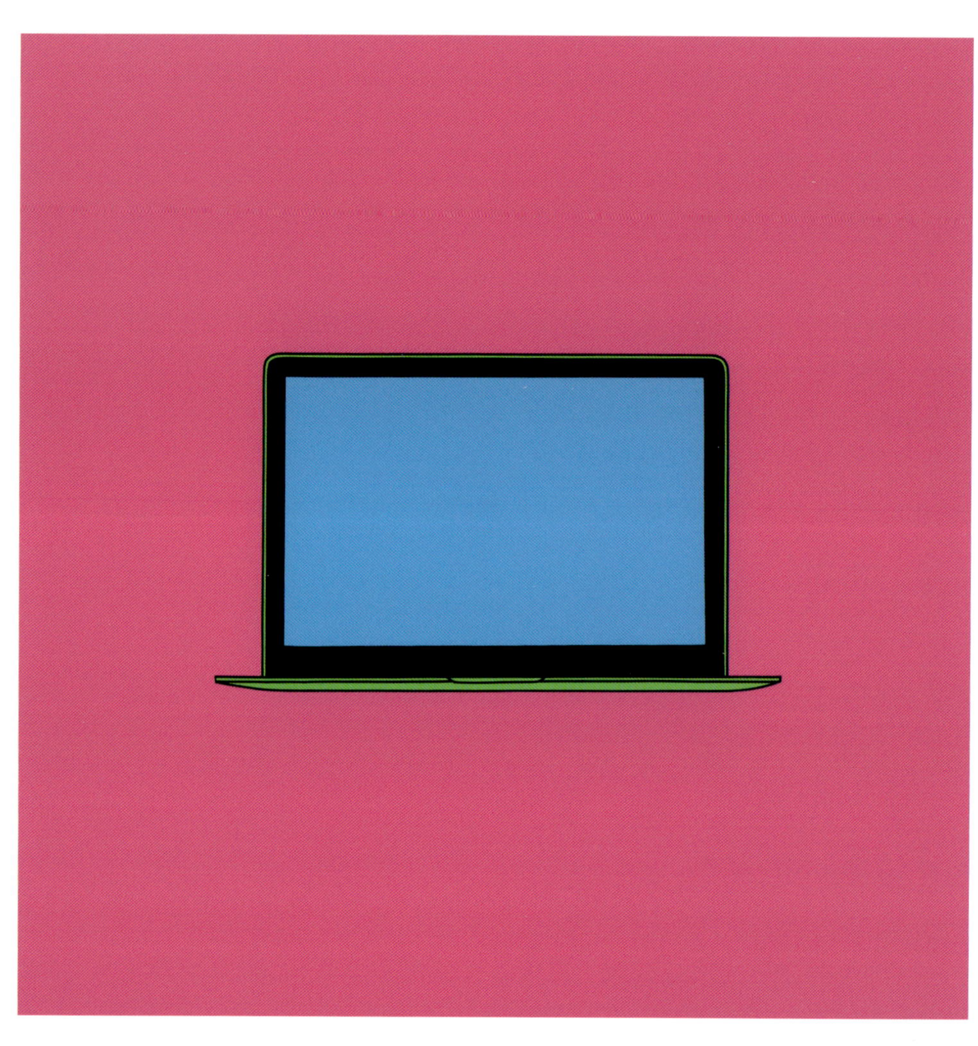

Untitled (laptop magenta), 2018
Acrylic on aluminium, 35½ × 35½ in. (90 × 90 cm)

Untitled (trainer fragment), 2017
Acrylic on aluminium, 24 × 24 in. (60 × 60 cm)

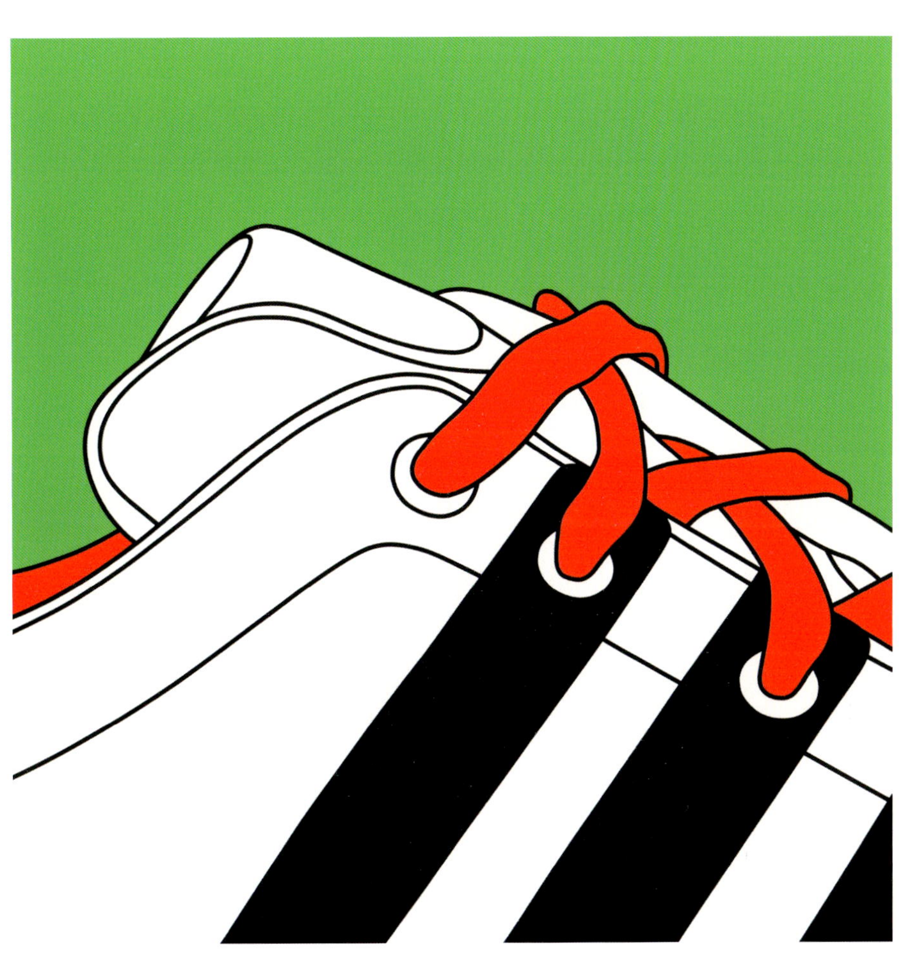

Untitled (guitar), 2018
Acrylic on aluminium, 48 × 48 in. (122 × 122 cm)

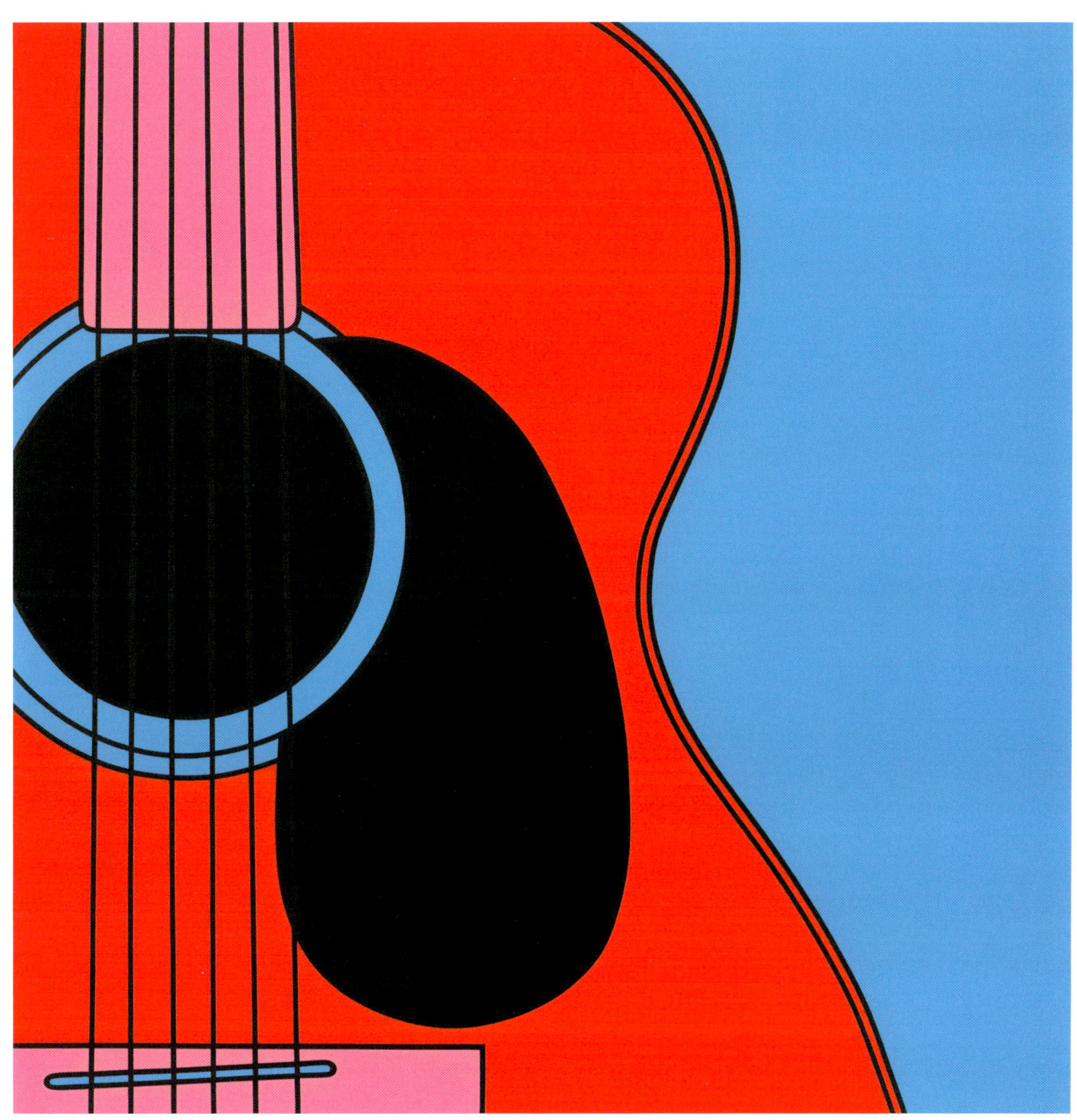

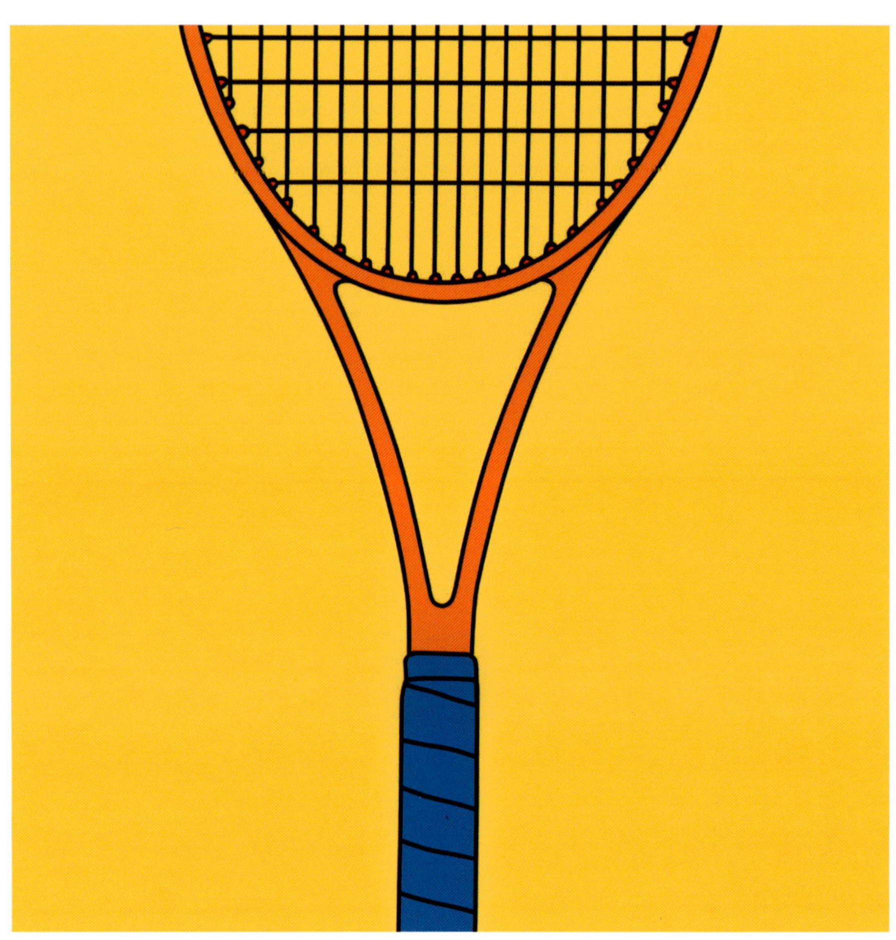

Untitled (tennis racquet fragment yellow), 2017
Acrylic on aluminium, 24 × 24 in. (60 × 60 cm)

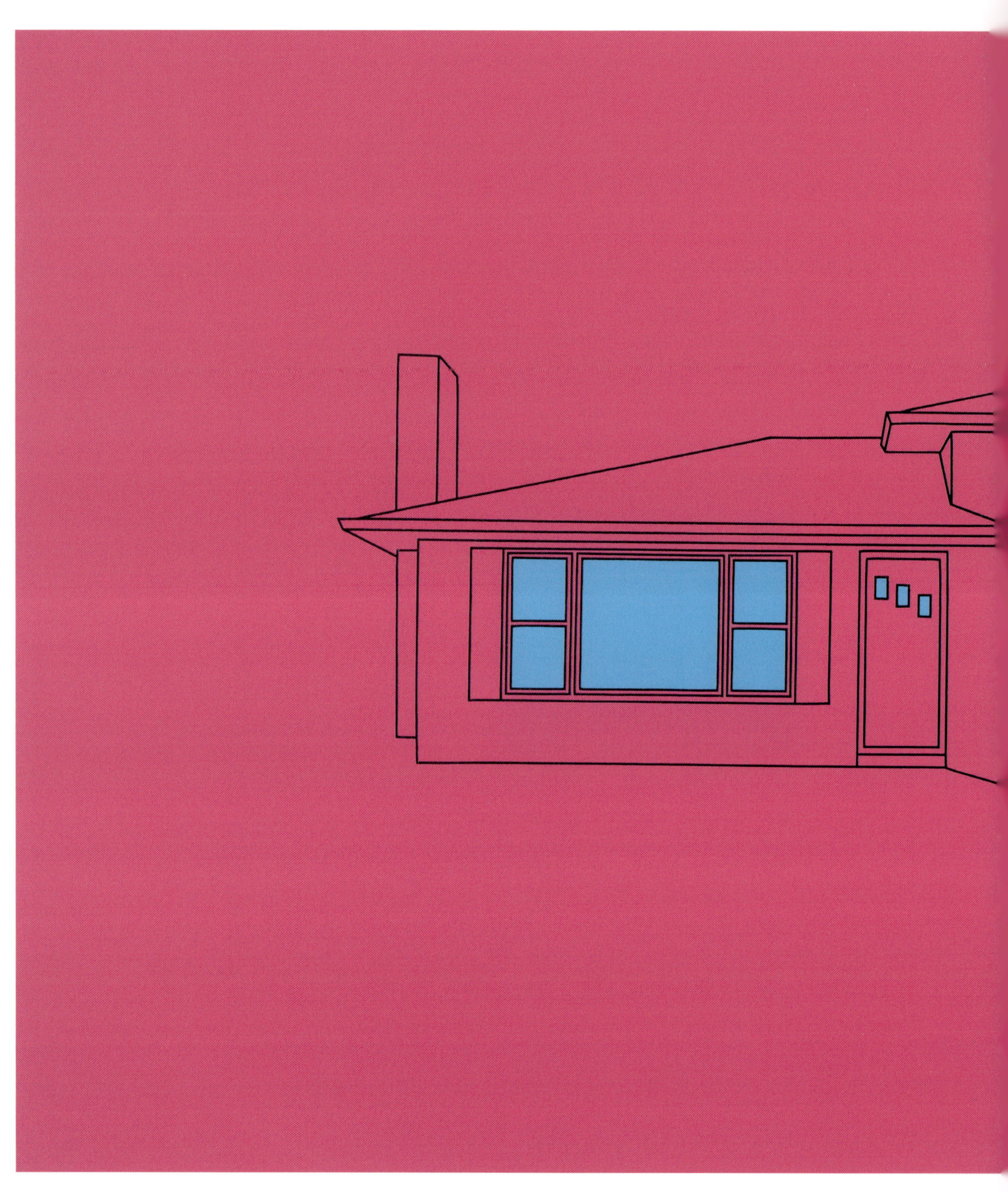

Untitled (split-level), 2018
Acrylic on aluminium, in two panels, 40 × 73¼ in. (102 × 186 cm)

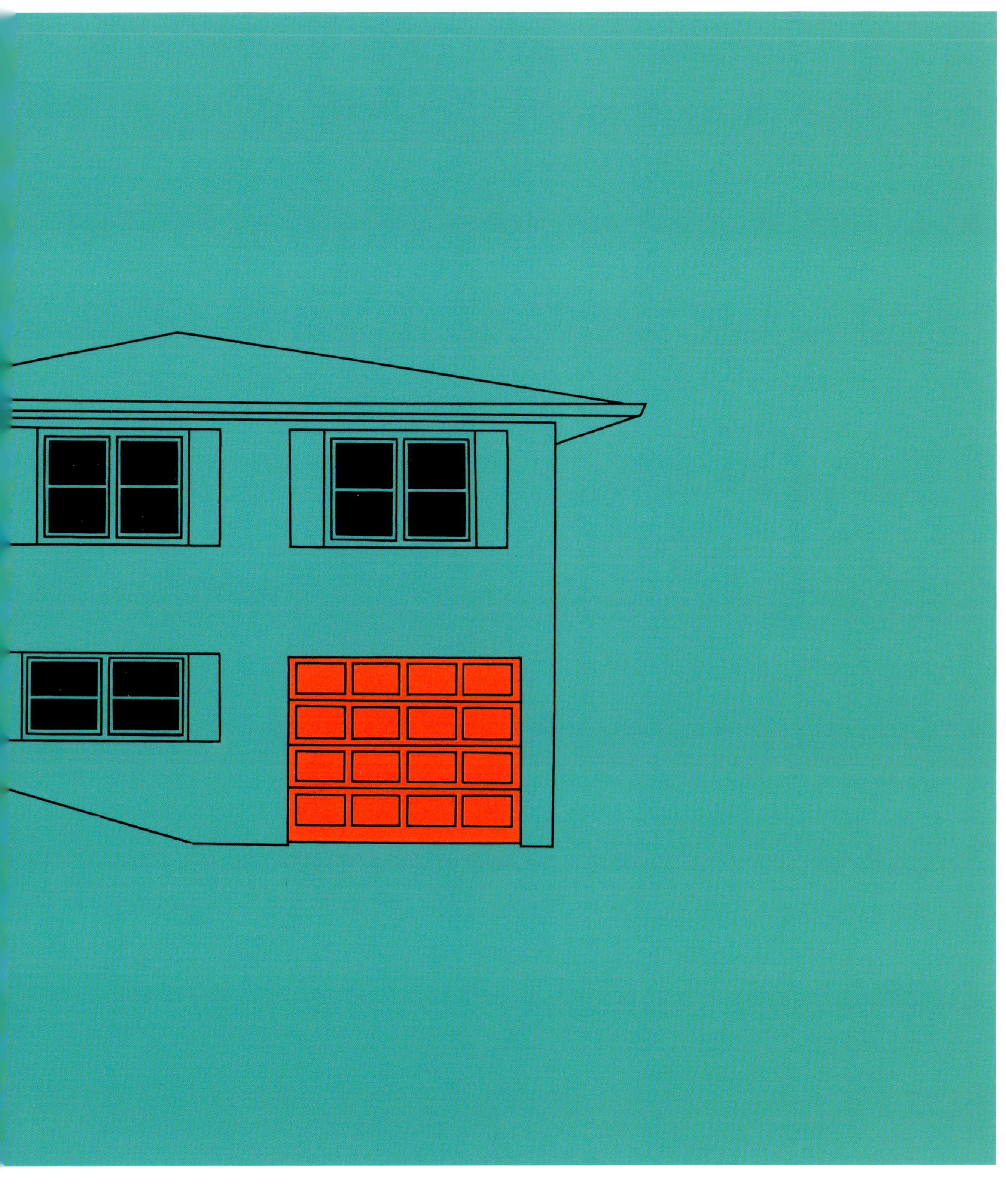

Eye Test, 2018
LED lightbox, acrylic, metal, 51 × 19½ × 4½ in. (130 × 50 × 11 cm)
Edition of 20

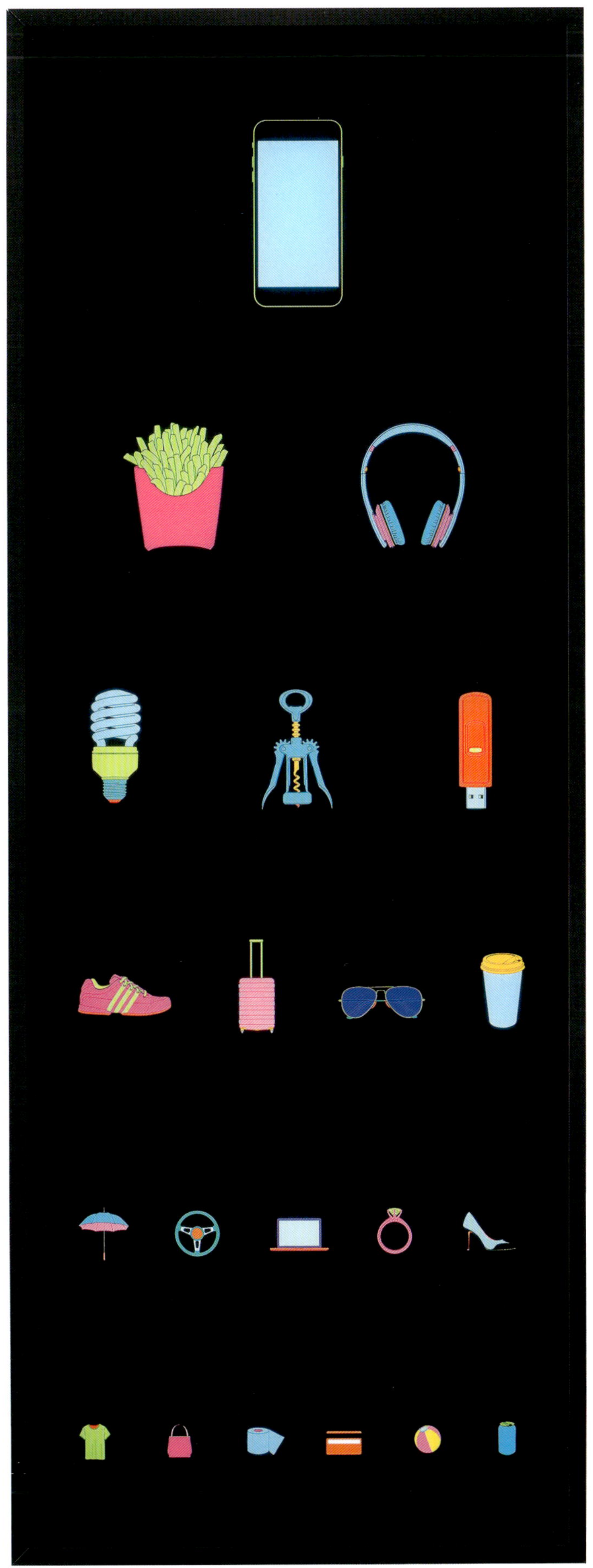

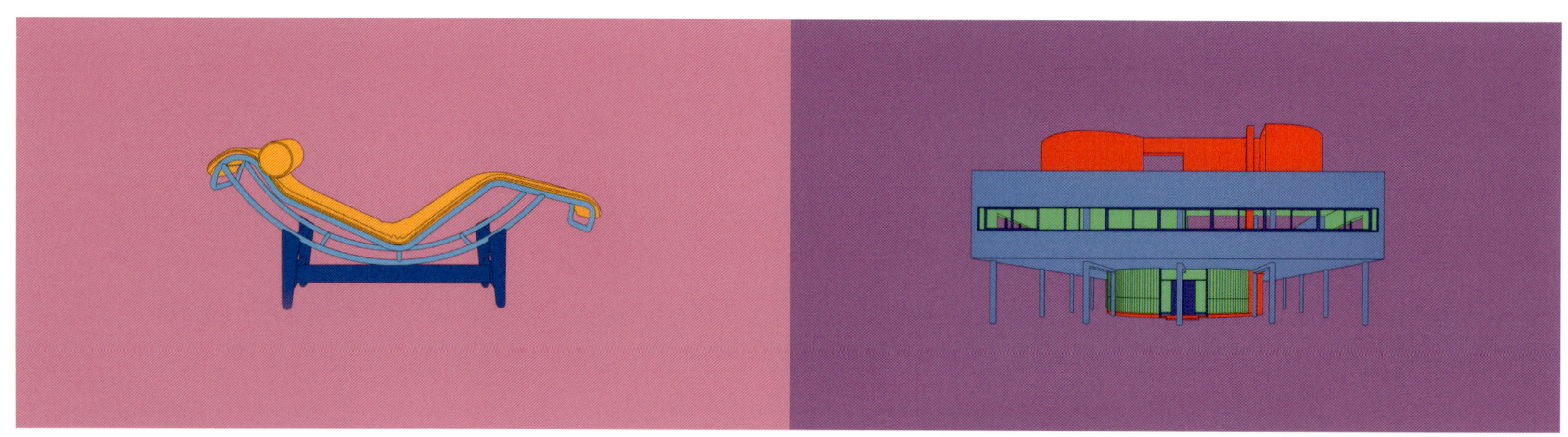

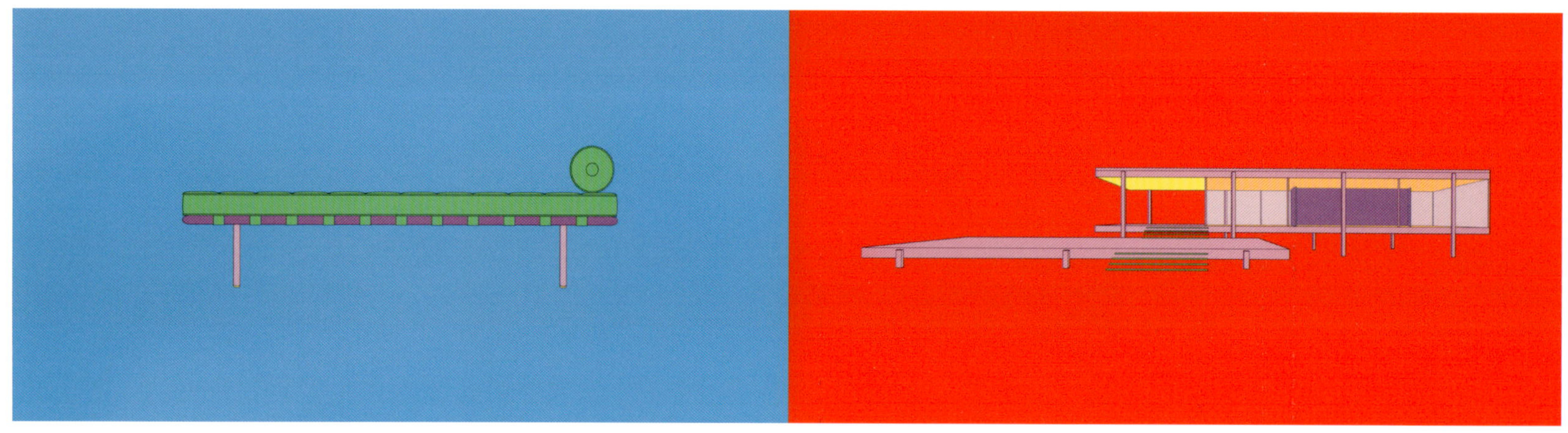

Design and Architecture, 2018
Silkscreen on paper, in two panels
4 prints, each 20 × 78¾ in. (50.9 × 200 cm)
Edition of 30

Le Corbusier
Mies van der Rohe

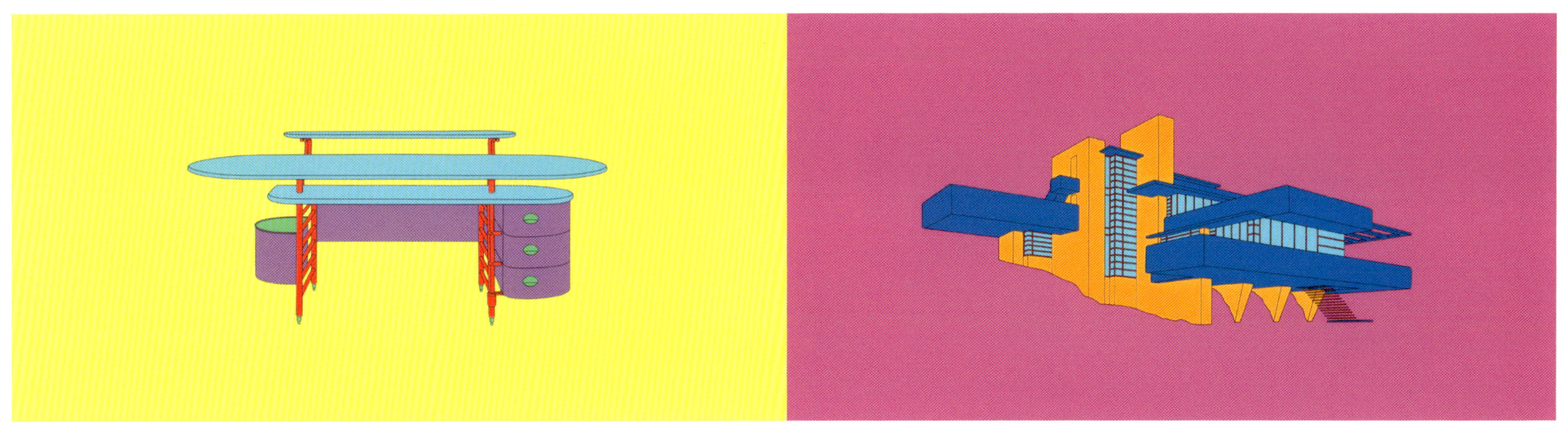

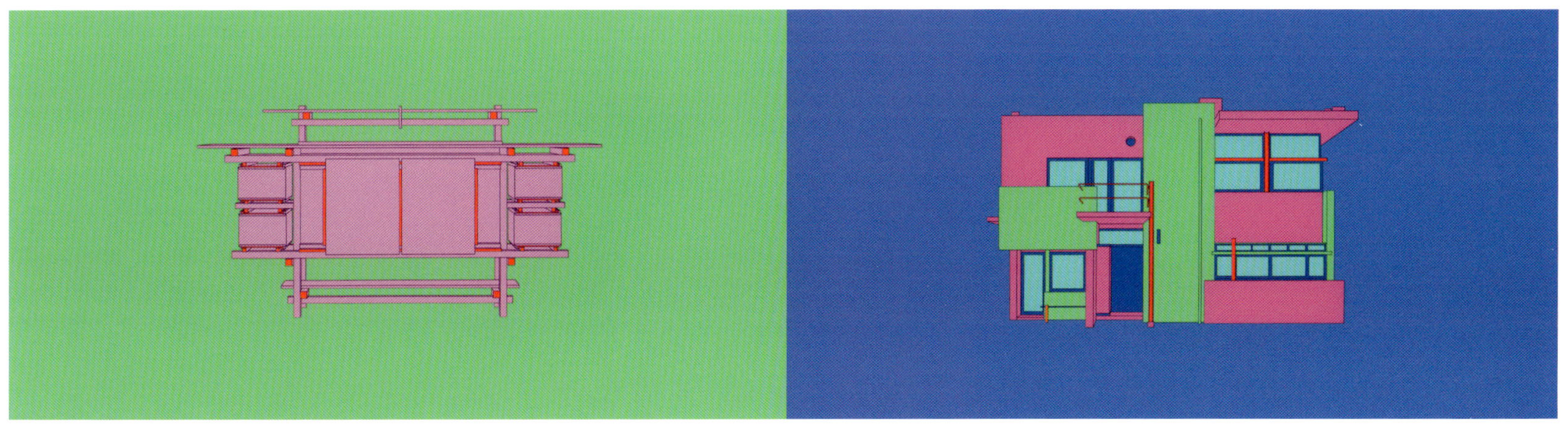

Frank Lloyd Wright
Gerrit Rietveld

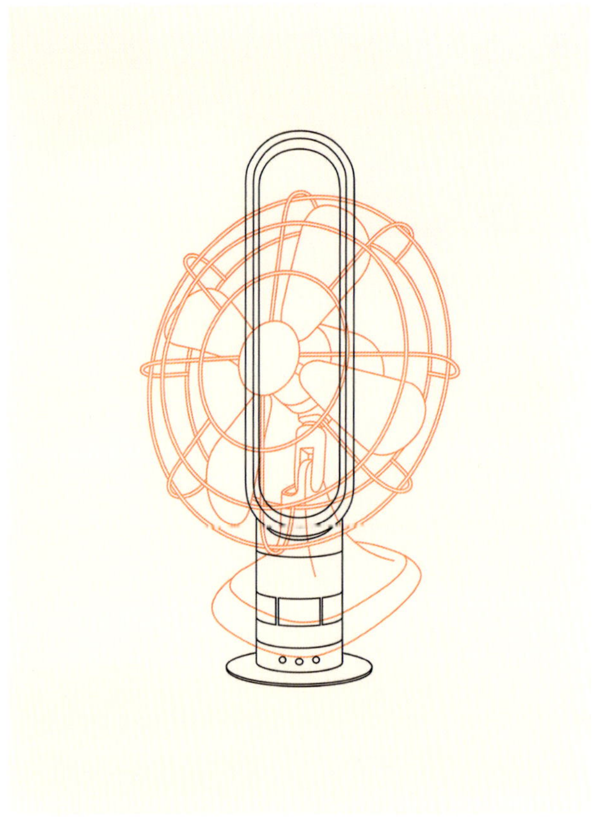
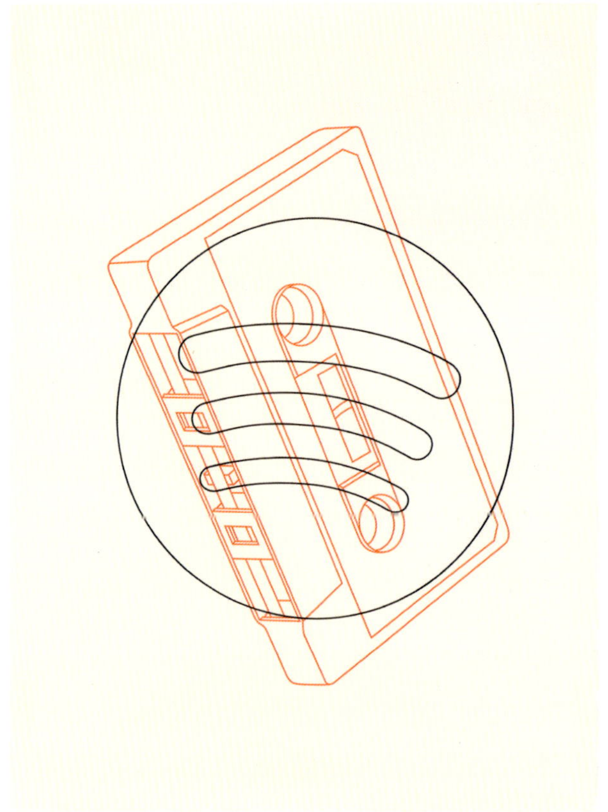
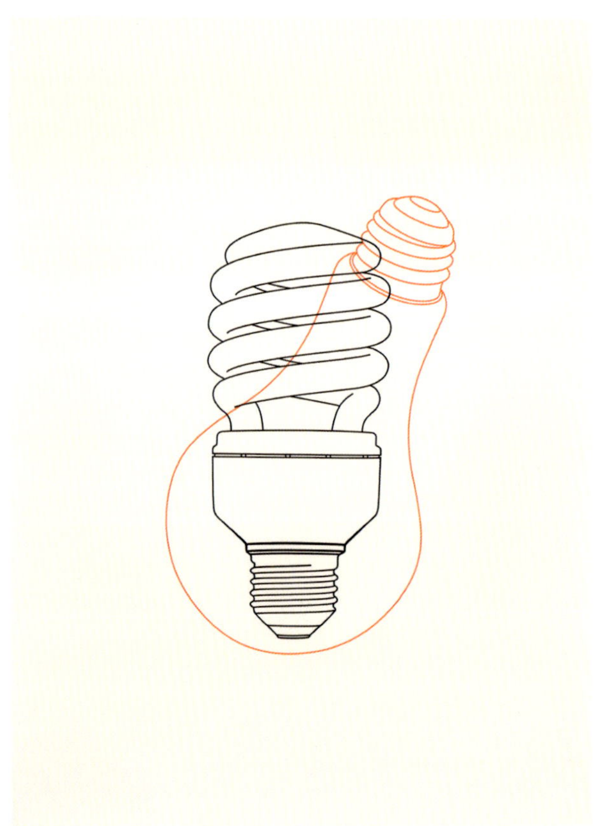
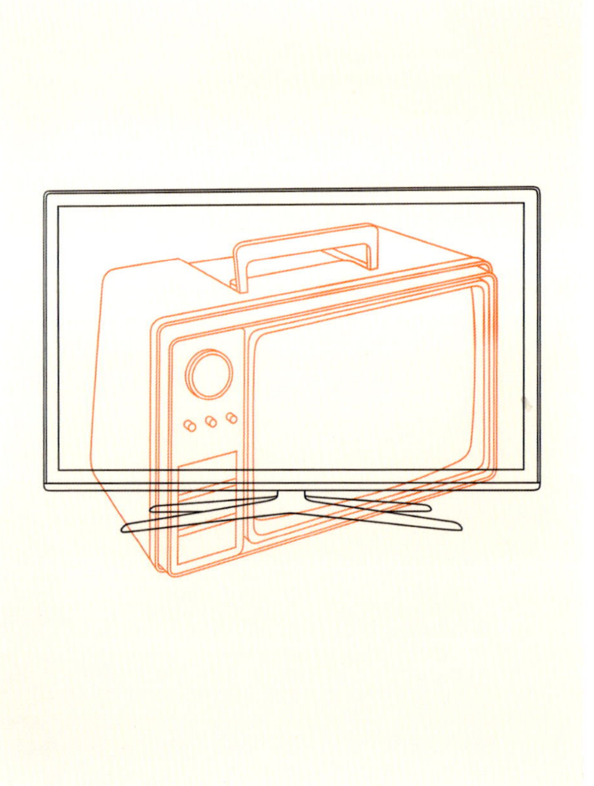

Then and Now, 2018
Letterpress on paper
8 prints, each 26¾ × 19½ in. (68 × 50 cm)
Edition of 20

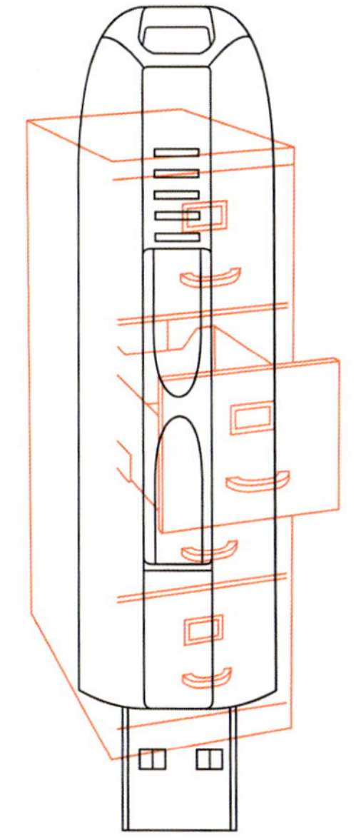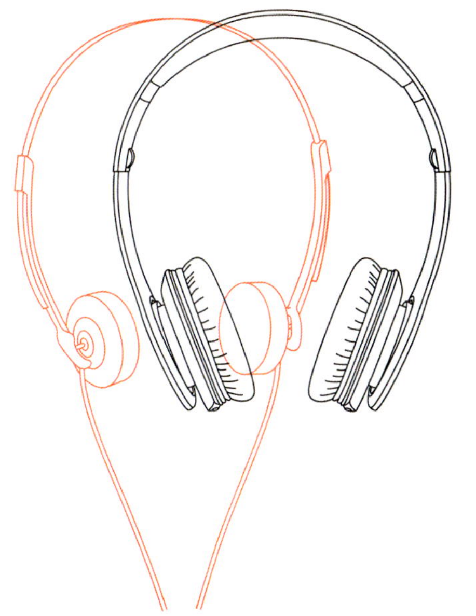

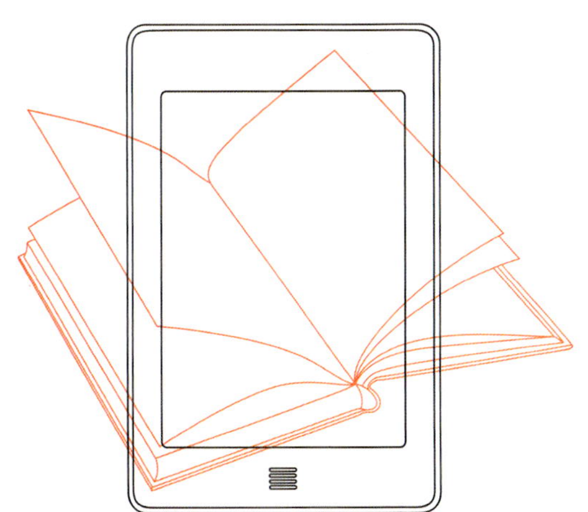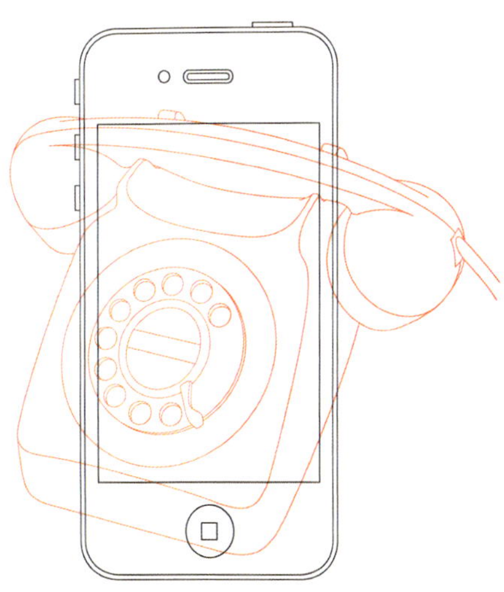

Fan/Fan; Cassette/Spotify; Filing Cabinet/Memory Stick; Wired/Wireless
Bulb/Bulb; Television/Television; Book/Kindle; Telephone/iPhone

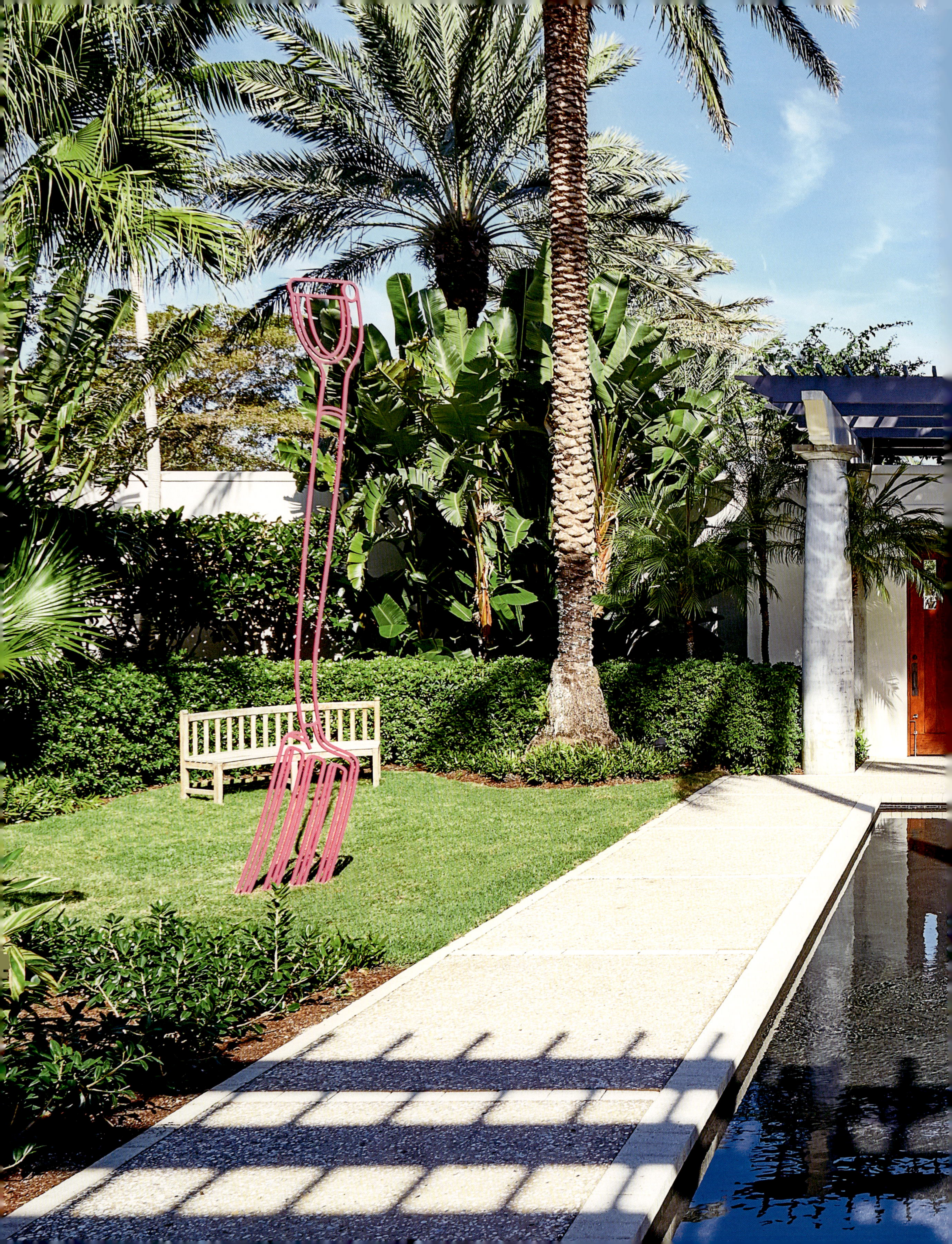

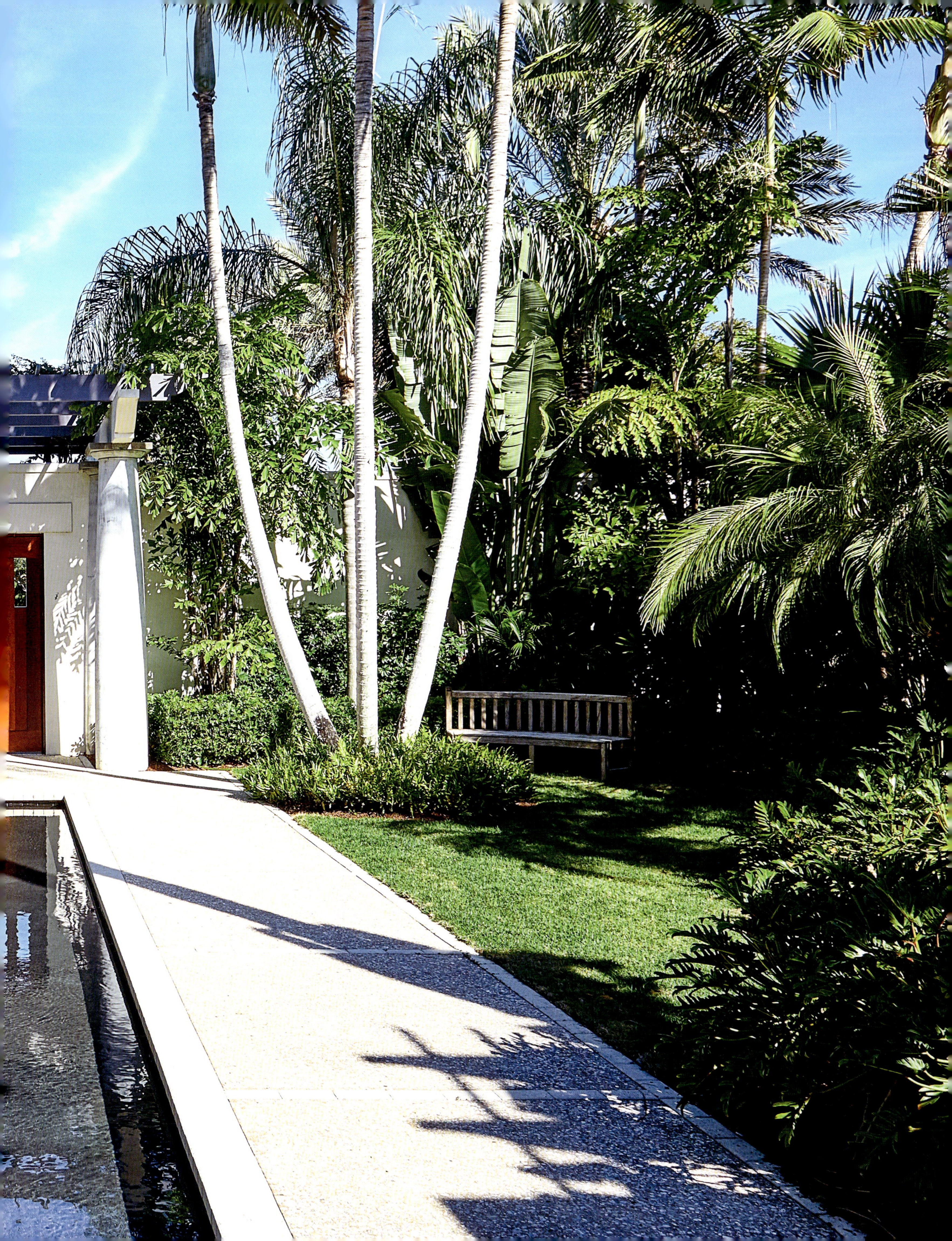

Previous pages:
Garden Fork (magenta), 2017
Powder-coated galvanised steel
157½ × 33 × 1 in. (400 × 84 × 2 cm)
Edition of 3 + 1 AP

Wheelbarrow (red), 2013
Powder-coated galvanised steel
100¾ × 193 × 1 in. (255 × 490 × 2 cm)
Edition of 3 + 1 AP

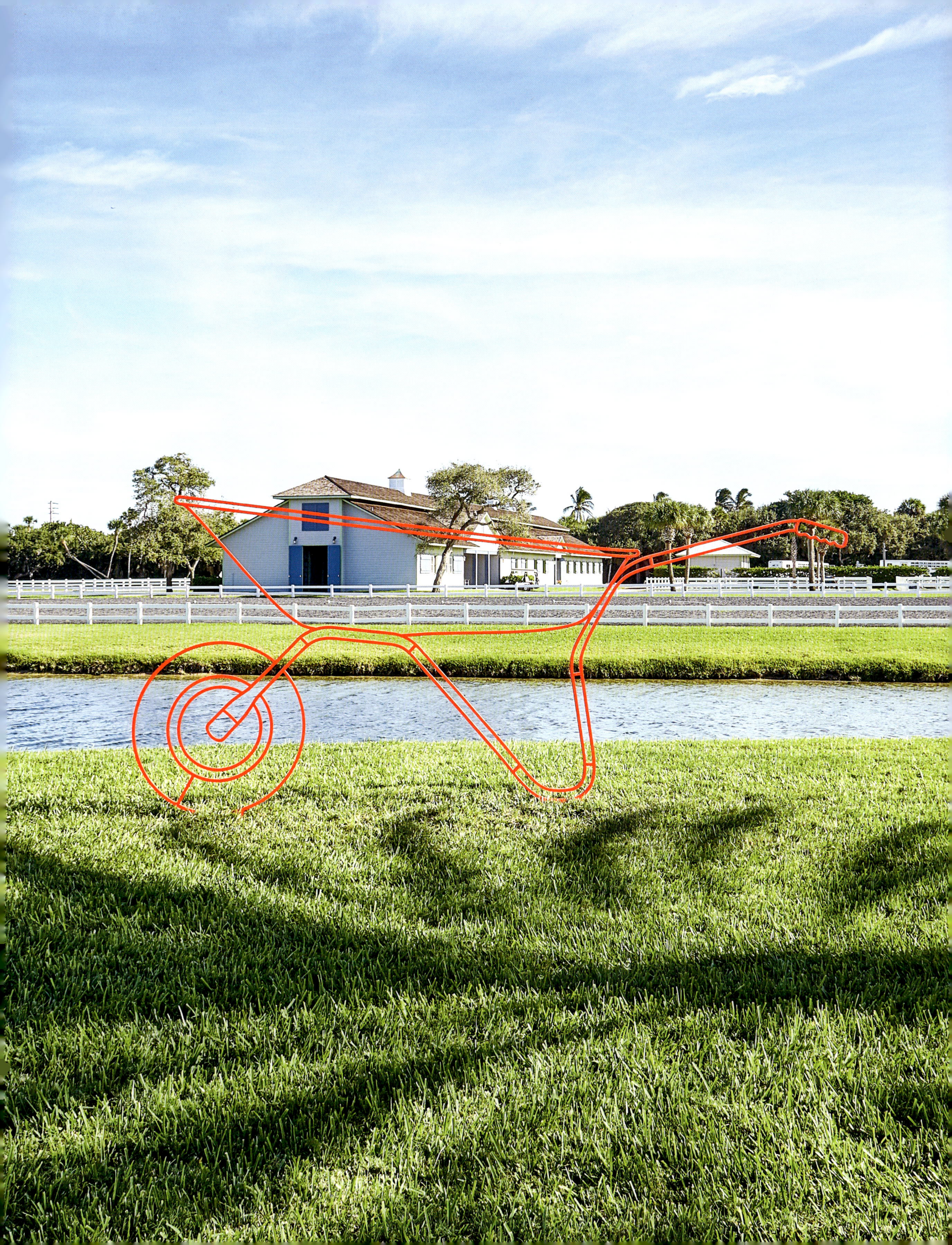

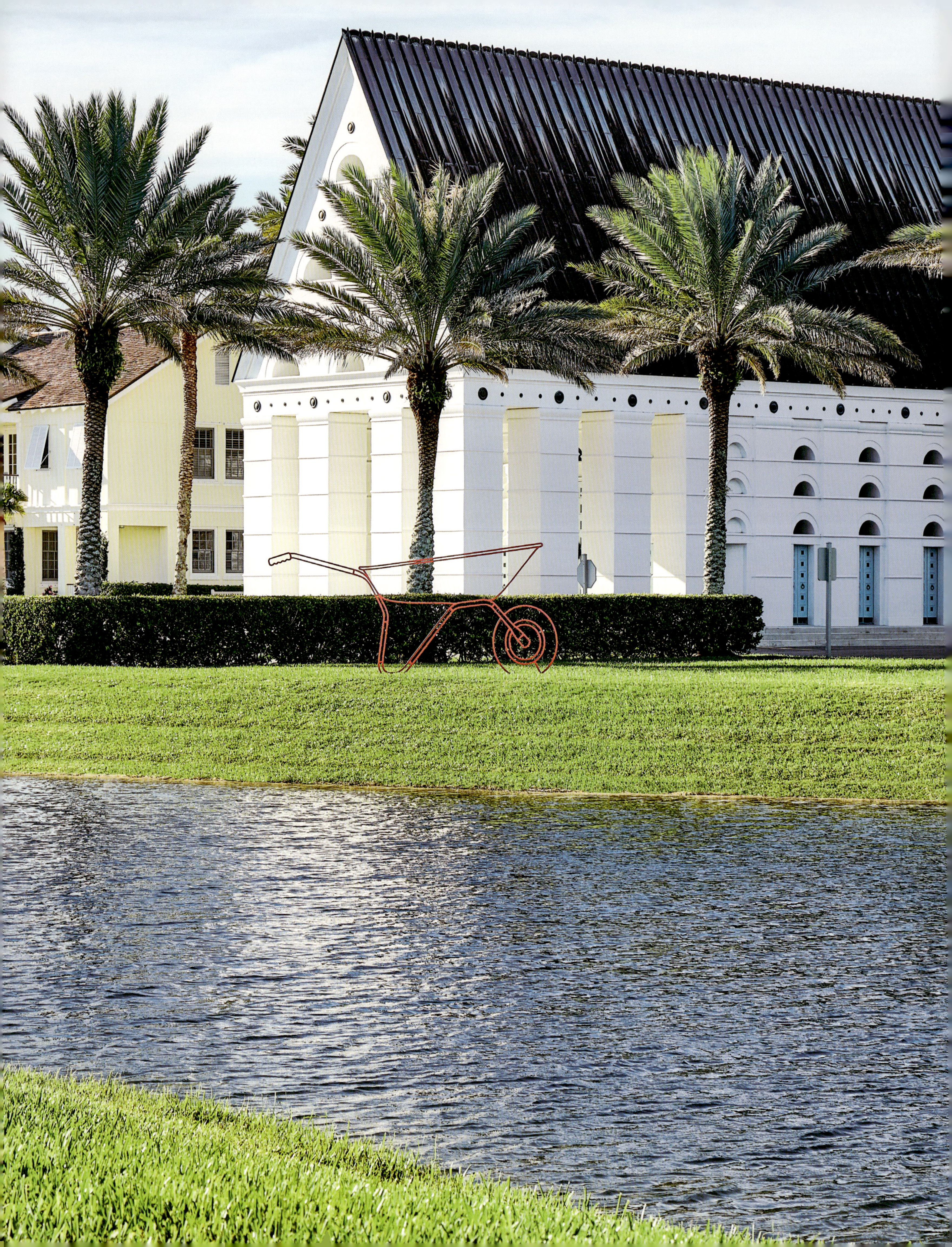

High Heel (pink), 2013
Powder-coated galvanised steel
133½ × 100¾ × 1 in. (340 × 255 × 2 cm)
Edition of 3 + 1 AP

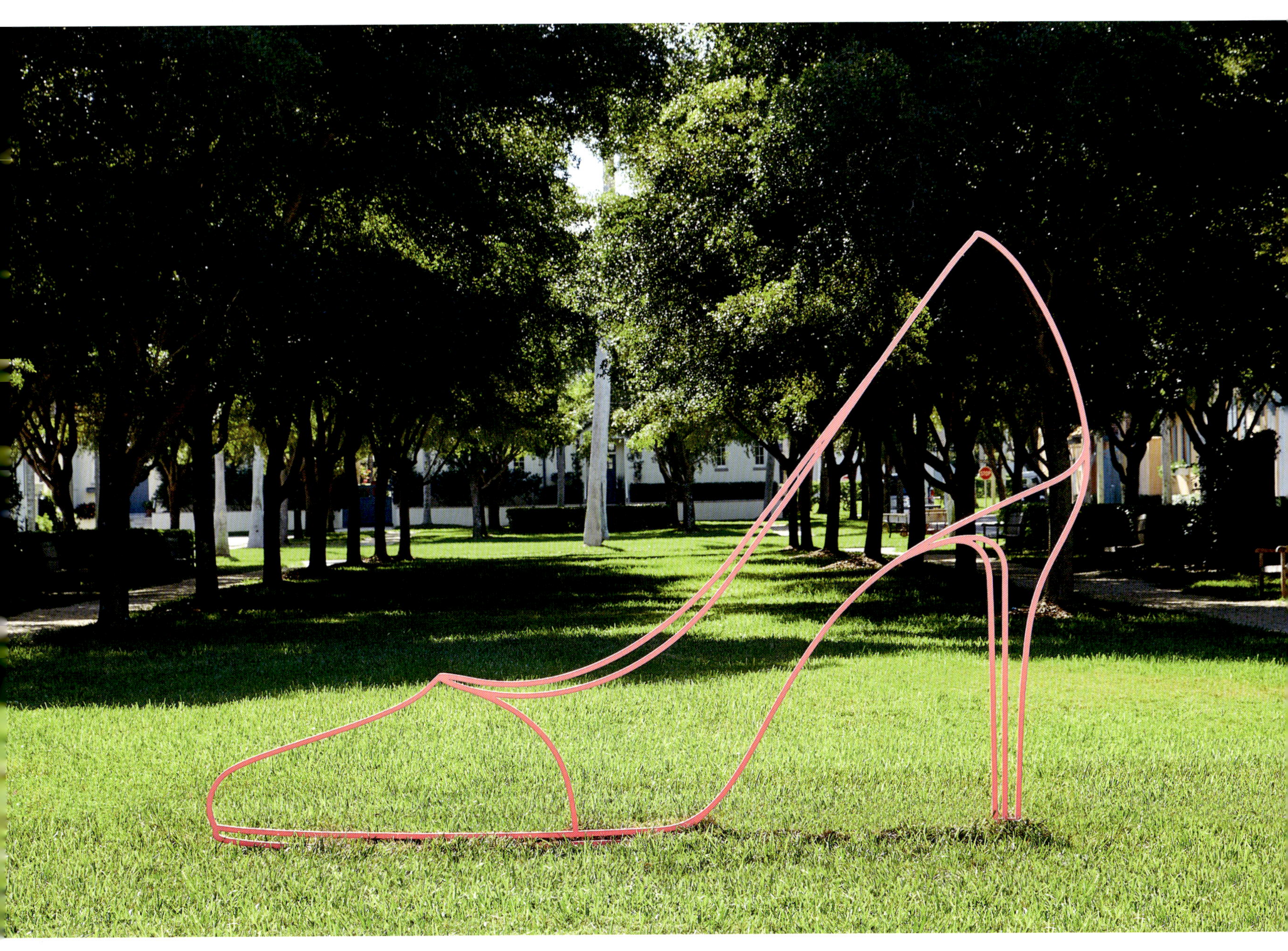

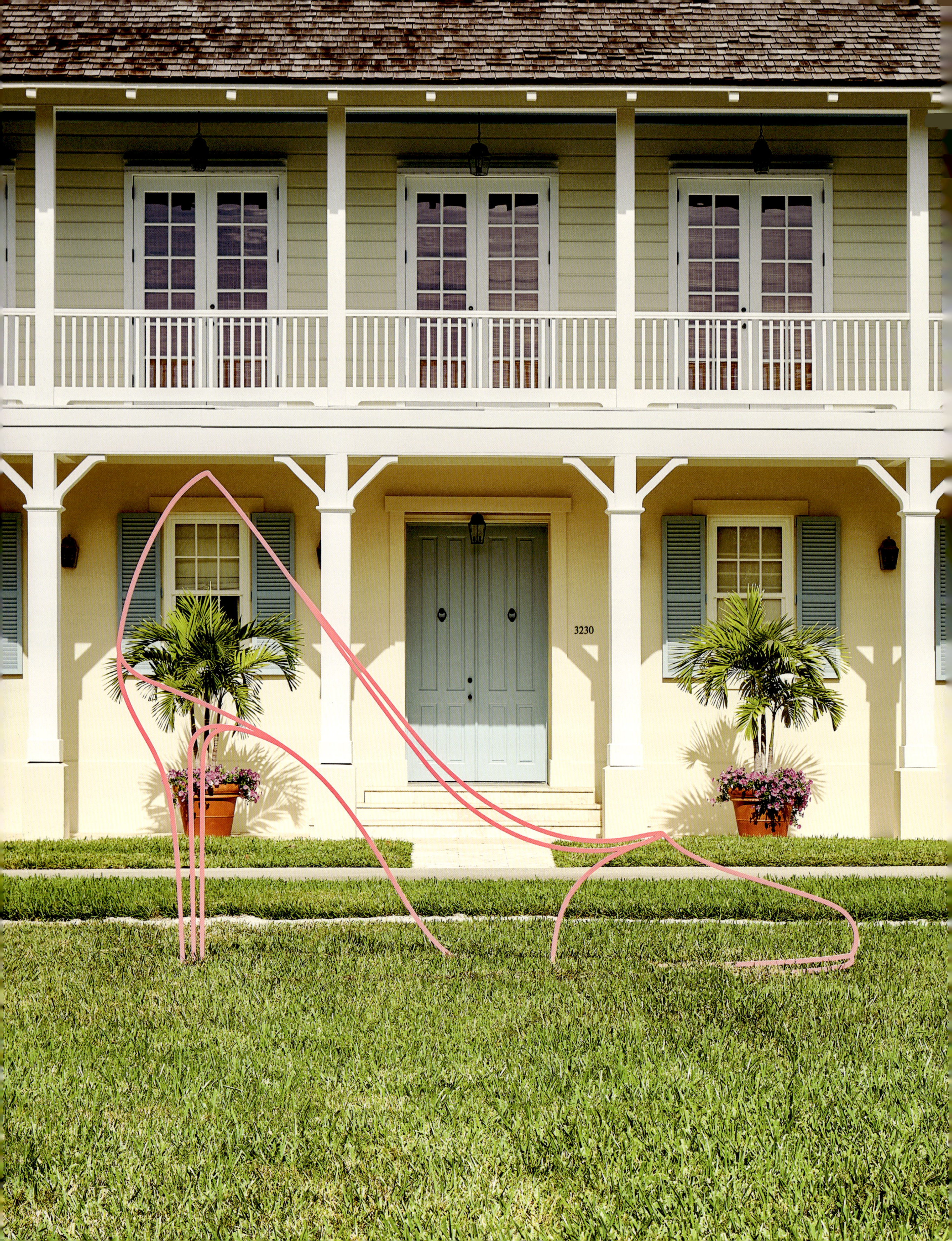
3230

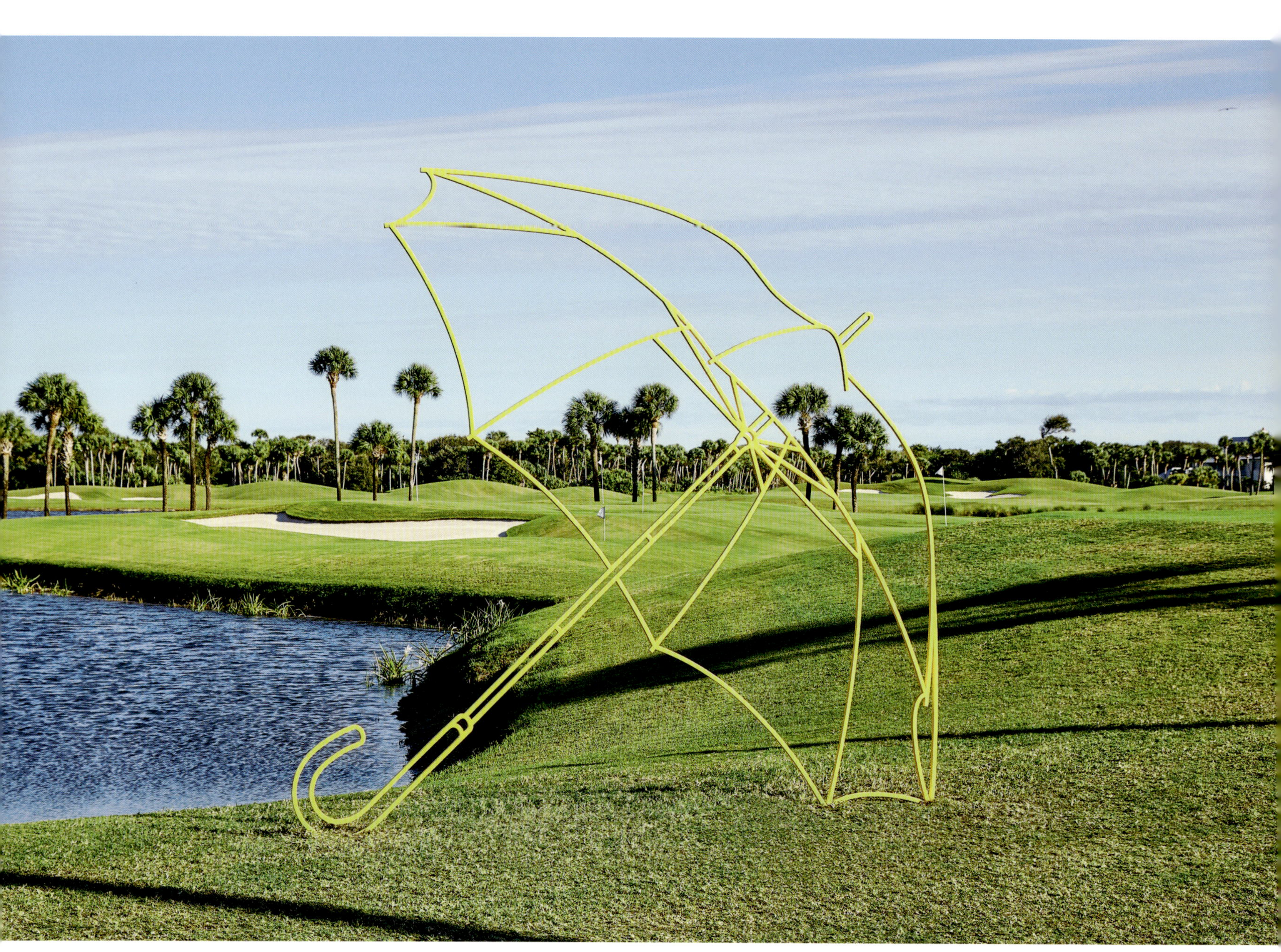

Umbrella (yellow), 2011
Powder-coated galvanised steel
119 × 128¼ × 1 in. (302 × 325.25 × 2 cm)
Edition of 3 + 1 AP

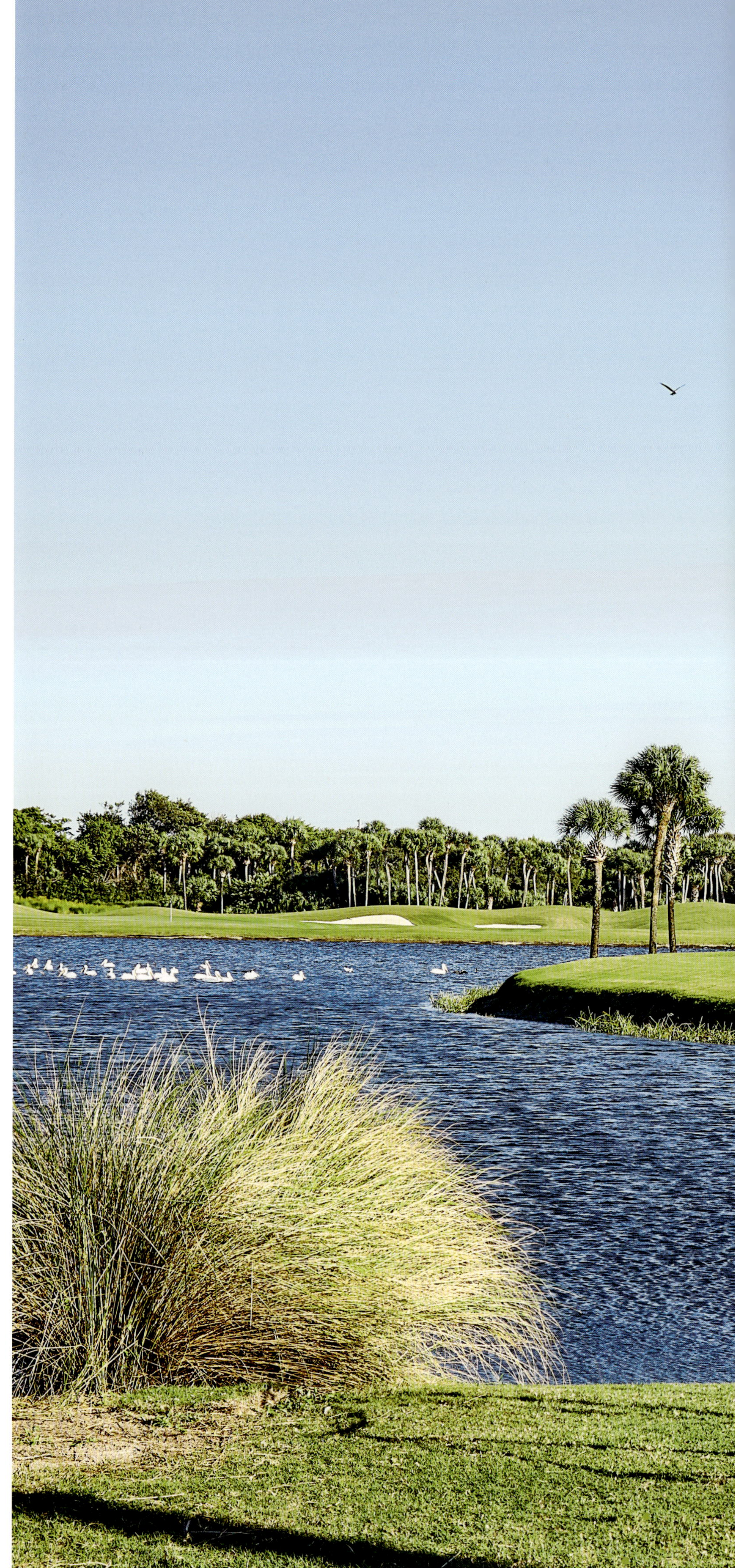

Umbrella (purple), 2013
Powder-coated galvanised steel
128¾ × 122½ × 1 in. (327 × 310 × 2 cm)
Edition of 3 + 1 AP

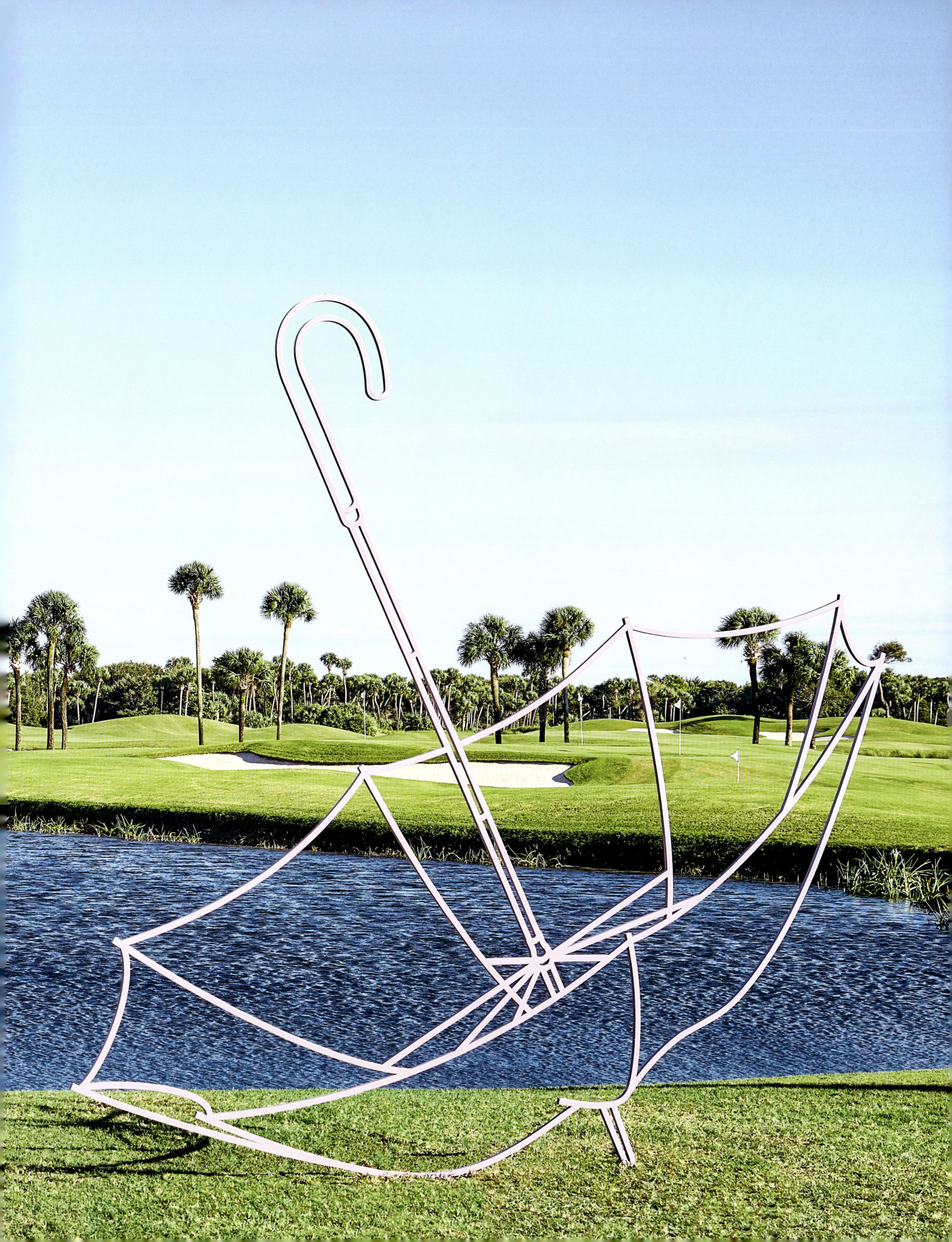

Bulb (magenta), 2015
Powder-coated galvanised steel
137¾ × 75¾ × 1 in. (350 × 192 × 2 cm)
Edition of 3 + 1 AP
Vero Beach Museum of Art, January 2019

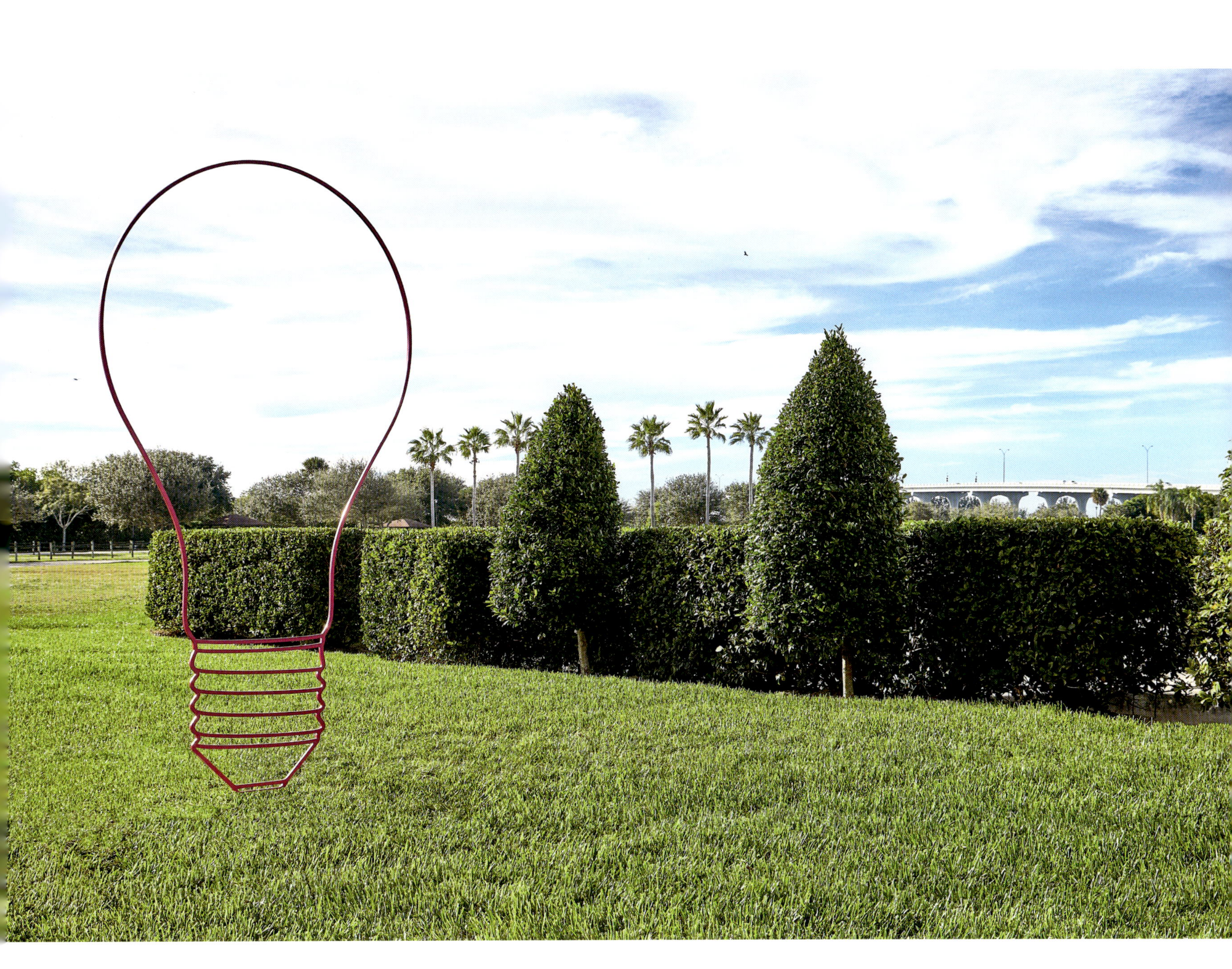

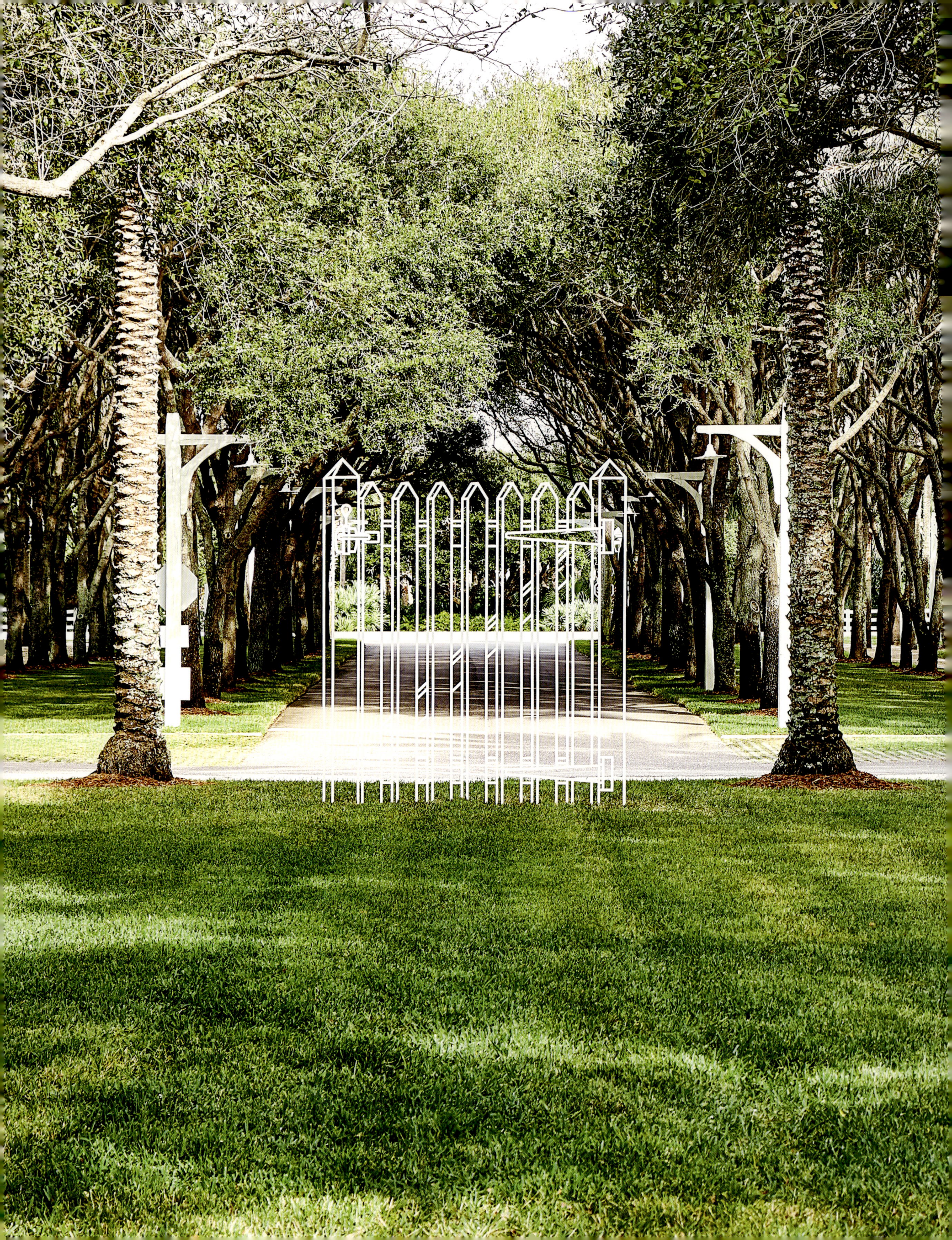

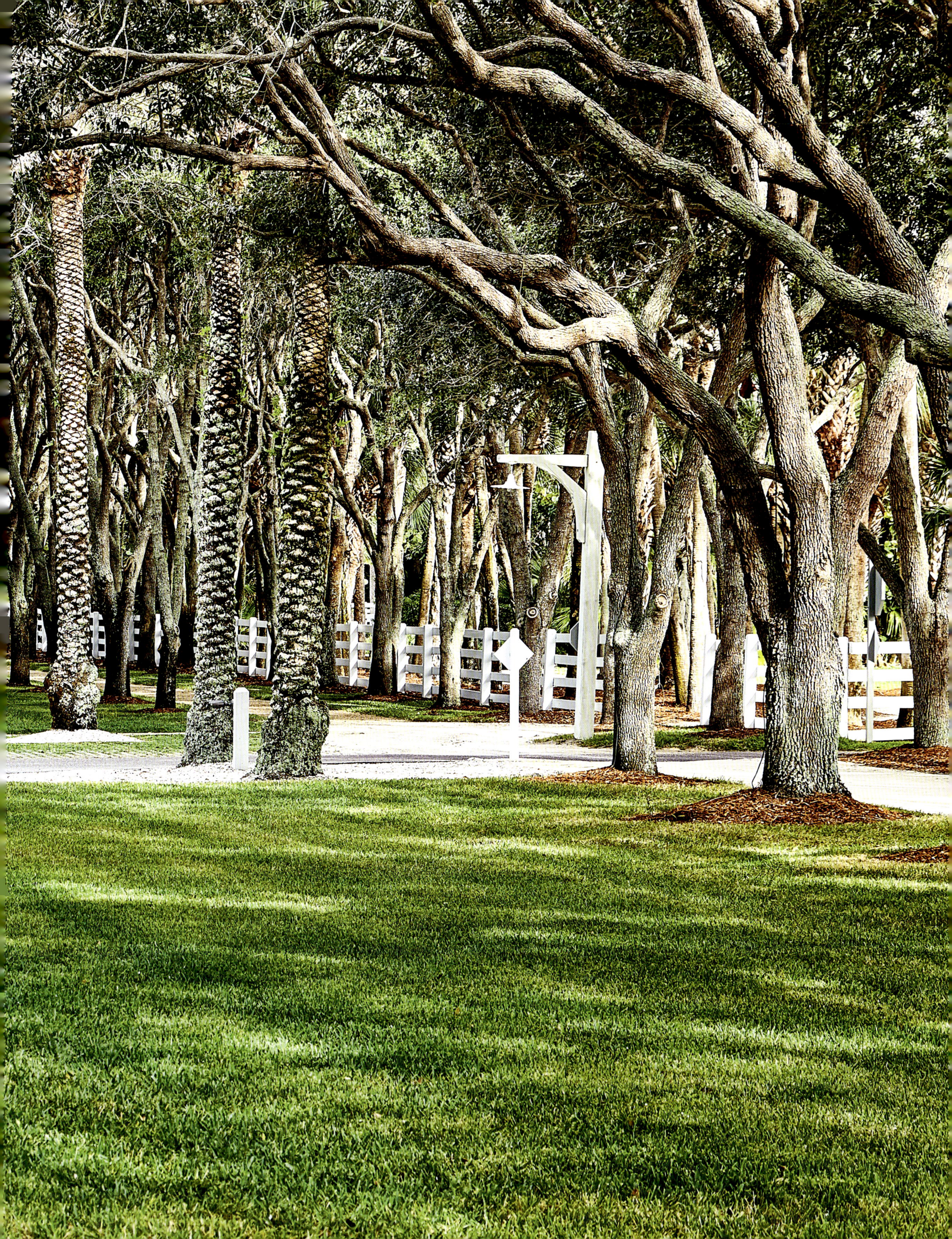

Gate (white), 2011
Powder-coated galvanised steel
116½ × 100¾ × 1 in. (296 × 256 × 2 cm)
Edition of 3 + 1 AP

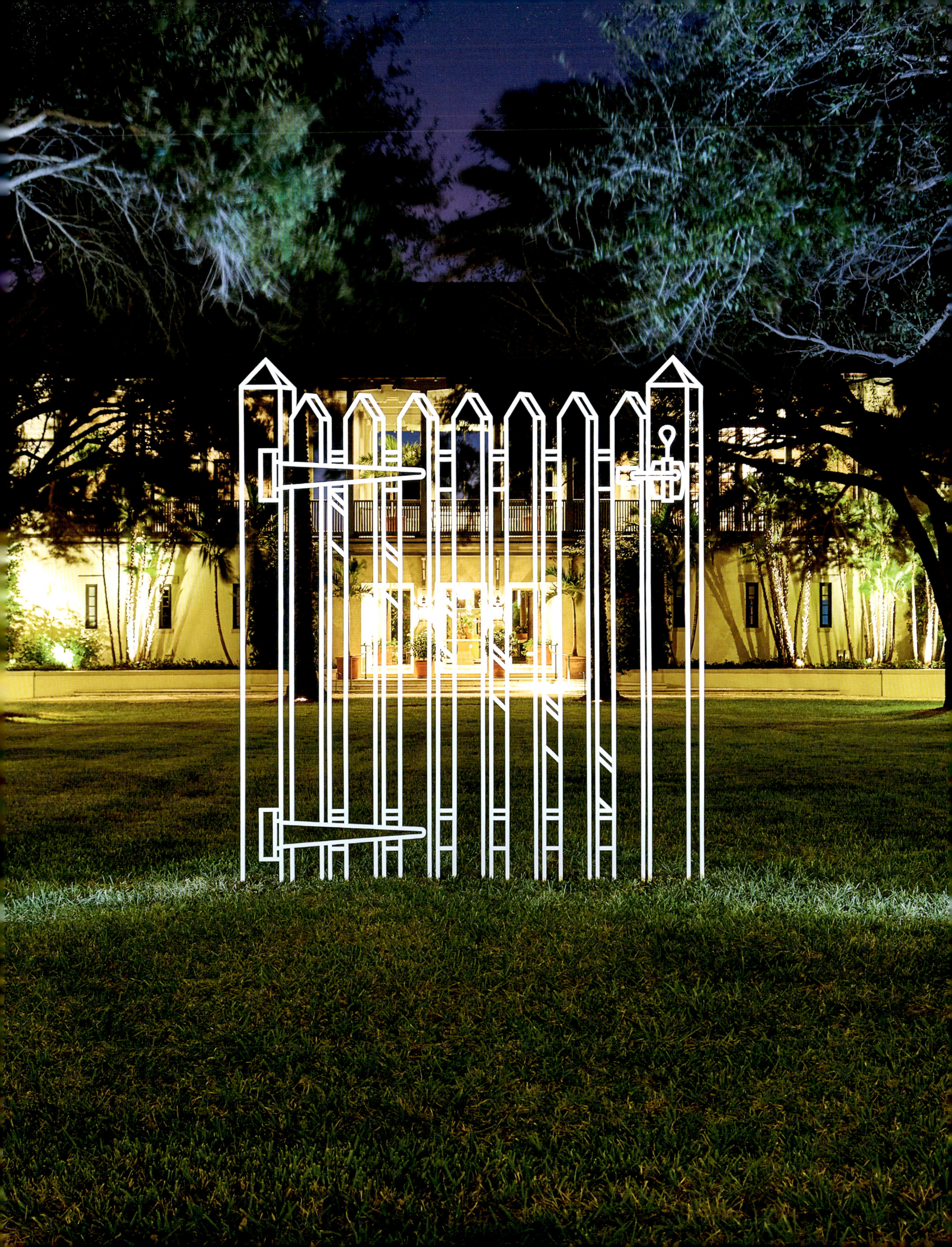

List of Works

Untitled (sunglasses fragment), 2017, p.8
Acrylic on aluminium
24 × 24 in. (60 × 60 cm)

Untitled (wireless), 2018, p.29
Acrylic on aluminium
98½ × 78¾ in. (250 × 200 cm)

Untitled (coat hanger fragment), 2018, p.30
Acrylic on aluminium
24 × 24 in. (60 × 60 cm)

Untitled (lightbulb blue), 2018, p.33
Acrylic on aluminium
35½ × 35½ in. (90 × 90 cm)

Untitled (American football), 2018, p.34
Acrylic on aluminium
24 × 24 in. (60 × 60 cm)

Untitled (stiletto), 2018, p.37
Acrylic on aluminium
48 × 48 in. (122 × 122 cm)

Double Take (iPhone), 2018, pp.38–39
Acrylic on aluminium, in two panels
35½ × 71 in. (90 × 180 cm)

Untitled (sunglasses), 2018, p.41
Acrylic on aluminium
48 × 48 in. (122 × 122 cm)

Untitled (dumbbell), 2018, p.42
Acrylic on aluminium
23½ × 23½ in. (60 × 60 cm)

Untitled (watch fragment yellow),
2018, p.45
Acrylic on aluminium
35½ × 35½ in. (90 × 90 cm)

Untitled (corkscrew fragment), 2018, p.47
Acrylic on aluminium
24 × 24 in. (60 × 60 cm)

Double Take (trainer), 2018, pp.48–49
Acrylic on aluminium, in two panels
78¾ × 157½ in. (200 × 400 cm)

Untitled (credit card), 2014, p.51
Acrylic on aluminium
48 × 48 in. (122 × 122 cm)

Untitled (laptop magenta), 2018, p.52
Acrylic on aluminium
35½ × 35½ in. (90 × 90 cm)

Untitled (trainer fragment), 2017, p.55
Acrylic on aluminium
24 × 24 in. (60 × 60 cm)

Untitled (guitar), 2018, p.57
Acrylic on aluminium
48 × 48 in. (122 × 122 cm)

Untitled (tennis racquet fragment yellow),
2017, p.58
Acrylic on aluminium
24 × 24 in. (60 × 60 cm)

Untitled (split-level), 2018, pp.60–61
Acrylic on aluminium, in two panels
40 × 73¼ in. (102 × 186 cm)

Eye Test, 2018, p.63
LED lightbox, acrylic, metal
51 × 19½ × 4½ in. (130 × 50 × 11 cm)
Edition of 20

Design and Architecture, 2018, pp.64–65
Silkscreen on paper, in two panels
Edition of 30
Four prints, each 20 × 78¾ in.
(50.9 × 200 cm)

Le Corbusier
Mies van der Rohe
Frank Lloyd Wright
Gerrit Rietveld

Then and Now, 2018, pp.25, 66–67
Letterpress on paper
8 prints, each 26¾ × 19½ in. (68 × 50 cm)
Edition of 20

Fan/Fan
Cassette/Spotify
Bulb/Bulb
Television/Television
Filing Cabinet/Memory Stick
Wired/Wireless
Book/Kindle
Telephone/iPhone

Garden Fork (magenta), 2017, pp.6, 68–69
Powder-coated galvanised steel
157½ × 33 × 1 in. (400 × 84 × 2 cm)
Edition of 3 + 1 AP

Wheelbarrow (red), 2013, pp.71–72
Powder-coated galvanised steel
100¾ × 193 × 1 in. (255 × 490 × 2 cm)
Edition of 3 + 1 AP

High Heel (pink), 2013, pp.75–76
Powder-coated galvanised steel
133½ × 100¾ × 1 in. (340 × 255 × 2 cm)
Edition of 3 + 1 AP

Umbrella (yellow), 2011, p.78
Powder-coated galvanised steel
119 × 128¼ × 1 in. (302 × 325.25 × 2 cm)
Edition of 3 + 1 AP

Umbrella (purple), 2013, pp.80–81
Powder-coated galvanised steel
128¾ × 122½ × 1 in. (327 × 310 × 2 cm)
Edition of 3 + 1 AP

Bulb (magenta), 2015, p.83
Powder-coated galvanised steel
137¾ × 75¾ × 1 in. (350 × 192 × 2 cm)
Edition of 3 + 1 AP
Installed at Vero Beach Museum of Art

Gate (white), 2011, pp.84–85, 87
Powder-coated galvanised steel
116½ × 100¾ × 1 in. (296 × 256 × 2 cm)
Edition of 3 + 1 AP

Michael Craig-Martin

1941   Born in Dublin, Ireland
Lives and works in London, UK

Education

1964–66   MFA, Yale University, New Haven, CT
1961–63   BA, Yale University, New Haven, CT
1959–61   Fordham University, New York, NY

Selected Solo Exhibitions

2017   *Michael Craig-Martin: All in All*, Hyundai Gallery, Seoul, South Korea
2016   *Michael Craig-Martin: Present Tense*, Galerie Andres Thalmann, Zurich, Switzerland
2015   *Michael Craig-Martin: Transience*, Serpentine Gallery, London, UK
NOW, Shanghai Himalayas Museum, Shanghai, China; travelled to the Hubei Art Museum, Wuhan, China
2014   *Michael Craig-Martin*, Gagosian Gallery, Davies Street, London, UK
Michael Craig-Martin, Gagosian Gallery, Hong Kong, China
Michael Craig-Martin at Chatsworth, Chatsworth House, Derbyshire, UK
2013   *Michael Craig-Martin: Less Is Still More*, Museum Haus Esters, Krefeld, Germany
2012   *Michael Craig-Martin: Drawings*, Luther W. Brady Art Gallery, George Washington University, Washington, D.C.
2011   *Michael Craig-Martin: New Painting and Sculpture*, Roche Court, Wiltshire, UK
2010   *Michael Craig-Martin*, Gagosian Gallery, Athens, Greece
Michael Craig-Martin, The Goss-Michael Foundation, Dallas, TX
2009   *Michael Craig-Martin: New Works*, Galerie Haas & Fuchs, Berlin, Germany
2008   *Alphabets and Sunsets*, Alan Cristea Gallery, London, UK
2007   *A is for Umbrella*, Gagosian Gallery, Britannia Street, London, UK
2006   *Michael Craig-Martin: Signs of Life*, Kunsthaus Bregenz, Austria
2005   *Arp / Craig-Martin / Arp*, Arp Museum, Remagen, Germany
2004   *Michael Craig-Martin: Surfacing*, Milton Keynes Gallery, UK
2003   *Eye of the Storm*, Gagosian Gallery, West 24th Street, New York, NY

Selected Group Exhibitions

2018   *Do I have to draw you a picture?*, The Heong Gallery,
        Downing College, Cambridge, UK
        Summer Exhibition 2018, Royal Academy of Arts,
        London, UK
        The Classical Now, King's College London, UK
        Harbour Arts Sculpture Park, Hong Kong Arts
        Centre, Hong Kong
2017   Summer Exhibition 2017, Royal Academy of Arts,
        London, UK
        Folkestone Triennial, Folkestone, UK
        Frieze Sculpture 2017, Regent's Park, London, UK
2015   ArtZuid International Sculpture Route, Amsterdam,
        Netherlands
        Summer Exhibition 2015, Royal Academy of
        Arts, London, UK (co-ordinated by Michael Craig-
        Martin)
        *Sleepless: The Bed in History and Contemporary
        Art*, 21er Hause, Vienna, Austria
2014   *Post Pop: East Meets West*, Saatchi Gallery,
        London, UK
        What Marcel Duchamp Taught Me, The Fine Art
        Society, London, UK
2013   *New Acquisitions*, Scottish National Gallery of
        Modern Art, Edinburgh, UK
        Art Everywhere, various locations, UK
2011   *The Indiscipline of Painting*, Tate St Ives, UK
        The Moderns, Irish Museum of Modern Art, Dublin,
        Ireland
2009   11th Istanbul Biennial, Antrepo No.3, Tobacco
        Warehouse and The Feriköy Greek School, Istanbul,
        Turkey
2008   *Exquisite Corpse*, Irish Museum of Modern Art,
        Dublin, Ireland
2007   *Living in the Material World: 'Things' in Art of the
        20th Century and Beyond*, The National Art Center,
        Tokyo, Japan
2006   6th Shanghai Biennale, China
        How to Improve the World: 60 Years of British Art,
        Hayward Gallery, London, UK
2004   *100 Artists See God*, Laguna Art Museum, CA;
        travelled to Institute of Contemporary Arts,
        London, UK
2002   *Passenger*, Astrup Fearnley Museum, Oslo, Norway
        Blast to Freeze: British Art in the 20th Century,
        Kunstmuseum Wolfsburg, Germany

Commissions

2017   *Palm Beach Parade*, Cityplace, West Palm Beach, FL
        Bright Idea, The Peninsula, Hong Kong
        Lexicon, Bloomberg Headquarters, London, UK
2010   *KIDS*, Radcliffe Children's Hospital, Oxford, UK
2009   *Street Life*, Docklands Light Railway Station,
        Woolwich Arsenal, London, UK
2008   *One World and Parade*, European Investment Bank,
        Luxembourg
2007   *Cascades*, Nice, France
2003   *Large Fan*, Regents Place, London, UK
2002   Norddeutsche Landesbank Headquarters,
        Hannover, Germany
        Laban Dance Centre, London, UK
1999   *Swiss Light*, Tate, London, UK

Public Collections

Arp Museum, Remagen, Germany
Arts Council Collection, UK
Australian National Gallery, Canberra, Australia
Baltimore Museum of Art, MD
British Council Collection, UK
Budapest Museum of Contemporary Art, Prague
Centre Georges Pompidou, Paris, France
Fitzwilliam Museum, Cambridge, UK
FRAC Nord Pas de Calais, Calais, France
Harvard Art Museums, Cambridge, MA
Leeds City Art Gallery, UK
Museum of Modern Art, New York, NY
Museo Nacional Centro de Arte Reina Sofia, Madrid,
Spain
Queensland Art Gallery/Gallery of Modern Art,
Brisbane, Australia
Southampton City Art Gallery, UK
Tate Collection, London, UK
Victoria & Albert Museum, London, UK
Walker Art Gallery, Liverpool, UK

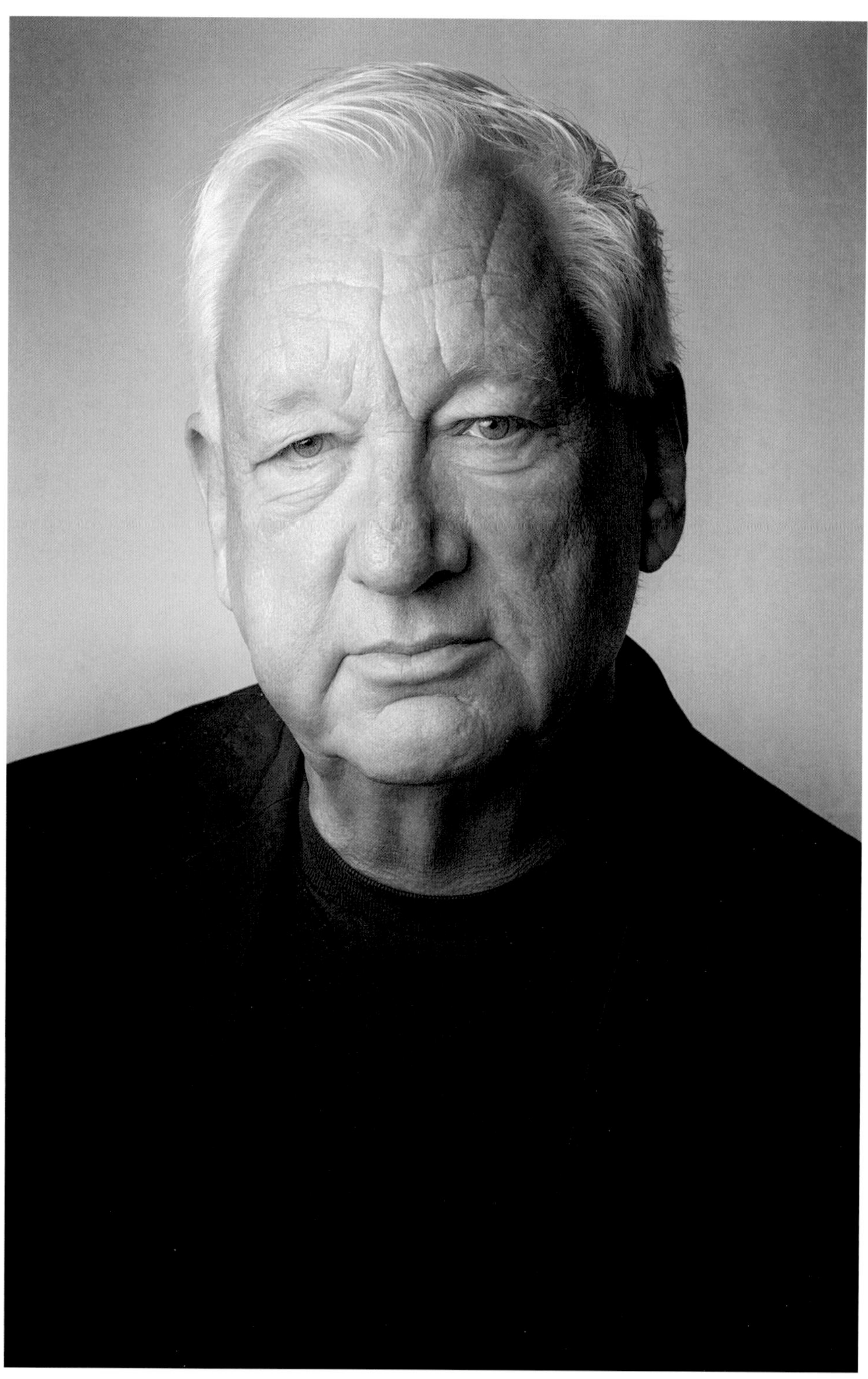

Michael Craig-Martin (photo Caroline True)

First published in 2019 by

Windsor Press
3125 Windsor Boulevard
Vero Beach
FL 32963

Royal Academy of Arts
Burlington House
Piccadilly
London
W1J 0BD

On the occasion of the exhibition

Michael Craig-Martin: Present Sense
29 January–25 April 2019

The Gallery at Windsor
3125 Windsor Boulevard
Vero Beach
FL 32963
www.windsorflorida.com/gallery

All images © Michael Craig-Martin, 2019
Courtesy of Gagosian and Alan Cristea
Gallery

Photography credits
Aric Attas, pp.6, 18–19, 68–69, 71, 72, 75, 76,
78, 80–81, 83, 84–85, 87
Mike Bruce, pp.8, 10, 29, 30, 33, 34, 37,
38–39, 41, 42, 45, 47, 48–49, 51, 52, 55, 57,
58, 60–61
© The Josef and Anni Albers Foundation /
DACS 2018, p.20
Peter White, pp.25, 64–65, 66–67
Jack Hems, p.63
Caroline True, p.92

'Michael Craig-Martin in Conversation
with Tim Marlow' © Tim Marlow and
Michael Craig-Martin, 2019
'Art in the Present Sense' © Ben Luke, 2019

Copy editing: Dorothy Feaver

Designed by Mark Thomson
Set in Unica77 and Lexicon

Printed in Belgium by die Keure
in an edition of 1,500 copies

Catalogue © Windsor Press, Vero Beach /
Royal Academy of Arts, London, 2019

British Library Cataloguing-in-Publication
Data
A catalogue record for this book
is available from the British Library

ISBN 978-1-912520-15-2

Distributed outside the United States
and Canada by ACC Art Books Ltd,
Sandy Lane, Old Martlesham, Woodbridge,
Suffolk IP12 4SD

Distributed in the United States
and Canada by ARTBOOK I D.A.P.,
155 Sixth Avenue, New York NY 10013

Acknowledgements

Sir Michael Craig-Martin

The Gallery at Windsor
Creative Director: The Hon. Hilary M. Weston
Art Gallery Manager: Laura Kelley
Marketing Director: Jane Smalley
Private Secretary to the Hon. Hilary M. Weston:
Louise Larlee
Marketing Assistant: Pat Palmer

Royal Academy of Arts, London
Series Curators: Christopher Le Brun PRA
and Tim Marlow, Artistic Director
Johanna Bennett
Elena Davidson
Joseph Green

Exhibition series coordinator:
Nicola Togneri

Gagosian
Larry Gagosian
Hannah Freedberg
Stefan Ratibor
Gary Waterston
Helen MacVicar

Alan Cristea Gallery
Alan Cristea
David Cleaton-Roberts
Charlotte Salisbury

Vero Beach Museum of Art
Director: Brady Roberts
Dana Twersky